The Gate Theatre presents

The UK Premiere

PURPLE HEART

By Bruce Norris

PURPLE HEART was commissioned by Steppenwolf Theatre
Company and the World Premiere was presented at
Steppenwolf Theatre Company, Chicago; Martha Lavey,
Artistic Director, David Hawkinson, Executive Director.
PURPLE HEART is produced by special arrangement with
the Playwright and Harden-Curtis Associates, 214 West 29th
Street #1203, New York, NY 10001

UK Premiere at the Gate Theatre on 28 February 2013

Supported using public funding by

**ARTS COUNCIL
ENGLAND**

PURPLE HEART
By Bruce Norris

Cast (in alphabetical order)

Grace	**Linda Broughton**
Thor	**Oliver Coopersmith**
Carla	**Amelia Lowdell**
Purdy	**Trevor White**

Creative Team

Director	**Christopher Haydon**
Designer	**Simon Kenny**
Lighting	**Mark Howland**
Sound	**Tom Mills**
Assistant Director	**Caroline Byrne**
Costume Supervisor	**Nicola Fitchett**
Production Electrician	**Dan Saggars**
Production Manager	**Bernd Fauler**
Company Stage Manager	**Kate Schofield**
Deputy Stage Manager	**Katy Munroe Farlie**
Dialect Coach	**John Tucker**
Fight Director	**Bret Yount**
Press	**Kate Morley** for Kate Morley PR (kate@katemorleypr.com | 07970465648)
Photographer	**Hugo Glendinning**

The Gate would like to thank the following people for their help with this production: Laura Glenn, Chris Hosking, the National Theatre, Piers Bishop from PTSD Resolutions, Becky Wootton and the Royal Court, Robert Kennedy at the Royal National Ear, Nose and Throat Hospital, Steppenwolff, the Gate Theatre's volunteer ushers, Duncan Russell at Yak-In-A-Box and all those who gave their help after this programme had gone to print.

Cover Image © Bill Owens (www.billowens.com)

Linda Broughton – Grace

Previous credits for the Gate include: *Sugar Dollies*. Other theatre credits include: *Roots* (Mercury Colchester & tour); *Home Death, The December Man* (Finborough); *A Day in the Death of Joe Egg* (Nottingham Playhouse); *2nd May 1997, I Like Mine with a Kiss* (Bush); *Ivanov* (Wyndhams Theatre); *The Chalk Garden* (Donmar Warehouse); *Snowbound* (Trafalgar Studios); *Hamlet* (The Factory); *The Safari Party* (New Vic Theatre, Stoke); *Racing Demon, Absence of War, Murmuring Judges, Galileo, The Crucible* (Birmingham Repertory Theatre); *Ballroom* (Riverside Studios & Tour); *When the Wind Blows* (Southwark Playhouse). In the 70s Linda was one of the founders of Monstrous Regiment. She is currently an Associate member of The Factory. Film credits include: *Babel, Bridget Jones's Diary, Sliding Doors, Watch That Man*. Television credits include: *Waking The Dead, Poirot, Carrie and Barry, Doctors, Silent Witness, Casualty, Paul Merton: Does China Exist? Hetty Wainthropp Investigates, Fist of Fun, Chandler and Co., Roughnecks, Knowing Me Knowing You, A Dark Adapted Eye, Men Behaving Badly*.

Caroline Byrne – Assistant Director

Directing credits include: *Shakespeare in a Suitcase* (co-directed with Tim Crouch for RSC); *The Recovery Position* (Lion and Unicorn); *Unrealistic Sleep Expectations, What Do We Do About Henry?* (Tristan Bates Theatre); *Twizzler Soaked Ecstasy* (SITI Co, Bernhard Theatre Studio); *The Children* (Embassy Theatre); *Lab Run, Attempts on her Life* (Durham Theatre, Berkeley, USA). As assistant director *King Lear* (RSC YPS Tour 2012).

Oliver Coopersmith – Thor

Theatre credits include: *The Physicists, Cryptogram* (Donmar Warehouse); *Cause Celebre* (Old Vic Theatre); *Henry IV Part 1 + 2* (Shakespeare's Globe); *The Ones That Flutter* (Theatre 503); *Blue Heaven* (Finborough); *2000 Feet Away* (Bush); *Macbeth* (Regents Park Open Air Theatre); *This is Progress* (ICA). Film credits include: *It's Alive*. Television credits include: *Case Histories, Grandma's House*.

Bernd Fauler – Production Manager

Bernd works as a freelance Production Manager on a variety of projects including theatre, contemporary performance/live art and dance as well as outdoor & site specific performances, having graduated with a First Class degree in Stage Management from Rose Bruford College. Previous credits for the Gate include: *The Trojan Women, Sunset Baby, The Prophet*. Other theatre credits include: *Roundabout London Season, Good With People, Wasted, 65 Miles* (Paines Plough); *Once Upon A Time In Wigan, Krapp's Last Tape, Spoonface Steinberg (Hull Truck Theatre); FAT* (Pete Edwards/ Lakeside Theatre); *The Fidget Project* (London Arts in Health Forum, Wellcome Trust); *The Bee Detective* (Tin Bath Theatre); *Access all Areas, Performance Matters 2011 & 2012* (Live Art Development

Agency); *SACRED 2009 &10 (Chelsea Theatre); London via Lagos* Season (Oval House Theatre); *Gross Indecency, Duckie @ Latitude 2010-12* (Duckie); *Hurts Given & Received, Slowly* (Wrestling School); *Where's My Desi Soulmate, It Ain't All Bollywood, Meri Christmas, The Deranged Marriage* (Rifco Arts).

Christopher Haydon – Director

Christopher is Artistic Director of the Gate Theatre. He studied at Cambridge University and trained at Central and the NT Studio. In 2007 he received both the inaugural Chichester Festival Theatre Heller Fellowship and the Channel Four Theatre Director's Bursary at the Salisbury Playhouse. He was formerly an Associate Director at the Bush Theatre and with On Theatre. Credits for the Gate include: *The Trojan Women, The Prophet, Wittenberg*. Other credits include: *Sixty Six Books, In The Beginning* (Bush Theatre/ Westminster Abbey); *A Safe Harbour for Elizabeth Bishop* (Southbank Centre); *Grace, Pressure Drop* - starring Billy Bragg (On Theatre); *Deep Cut* (Sherman Cymru/National Tour); *Monsters, Notes from Underground* (Arcola Theatre); *A Number* (Salisbury Playhouse); *The Stone* (RWCMD). He has co-edited three books: *Conversations on Religion, Conversations on Truth* and *Identity and Identification*. He has written for *The Guardian, The Scotsman, The New Statesman, The FT, The Independent* and *Prospect Magazine*.

Mark Howland – Lighting

Mark studied, briefly, at Oxford University prior to training in Stage Lighting Design at RADA. Previous credits for the Gate include: *The Trojan Women, The Prophet, The Kreutzer Sonata* (2012 revival), *Yerma, Wittenberg, The Kreutzer Sonata* (2009), *Vanya*. Other theatre credits include: *Hitchcock Blonde* (Hull Truck); *Ignorance* (Hampstead Theatre); *Canvas* (Chichester Festival); *Ghosts, Sweeney Todd* (Aarhus Theatre, Denmark); *Singin in the Rain* (New Theatre, Copenhagen); *Entertaining Mr. Sloane, One Flew Over the Cuckoo's Nest, Absurd Person Singular, Molly Sweeney, Translations* (Curve); *Measure for Measure* (Sherman Cymru); *Bea, Pressure Drop, On Religion* (On Theatre); *Six Dance Lessons in Six Weeks* (Vienna's English Theatre); *Dick Turpin's Last Ride, Much Ado About Nothing, Cider with Rosie, The Merchant of Venice* (Theatre Royal Bury St Edmunds); *Uncle Vanya, Dockers, The Home Place* (Lyric Theatre, Belfast); *A Number* (Salisbury Playhouse); *Topless Mum* (Tobacco Factory); *Monsters* (Arcola Theatre); *The Pains of Youth* (Belgrade Theatre).

Simon Kenny – Design

Recent theatre includes *Sleuth* (Watermill); *The American Season: Red Light Winter, In A Garden* and *In The Next Room or The Vibrator Play* (Ustinov Studio); *Good Grief* (Theatre Royal Bath and tour); *Island* (National Theatre); *Feathers in the Snow, The Busy Body, Someone Who'll Watch Over Me, The Belle's Stratagem,*

Antigone (Southwark Playhouse); *Hamlet* (Young Vic Taking Part); *The Mountaintop* (Derby LIVE); *RUN!: A Sports Day Musical*, *The Machine Gunners* (Polka); *Holes* (New Wimbledon Studio); *There's Only One Wayne Matthews* (Sheffield Crucible Studio); *Palace of the End*, *Riff Raff* (Arcola); *Pedestrian* (Bristol Old Vic); *Gross Indecency* (Duckie); *Tales from the Bar of Lost Souls* (imitating the dog/National Theatre of Greece); *Seven Jewish Children* (Hackney Empire); three national and international tours of new plays for British-Asian company Rifco Arts; *Woyzeck*, *Machinal* (Central School of Speech & Drama); *The Workroom*, *The Madras House* (RADA); *Legally Blonde: The Musical*, *Roberto Zucco* (Arts Ed); and as Associate Designer, *Double Feature* (National Theatre Paintframe). Opera credits include: *A Voice of One Delight* (McCaldin Arts/Tête-à-Tête); *The Cunning Little Vixen*, *The Prodigal Son*, *The Homecoming*, *Háry János*, *Orlando* (all Ryedale Festival); *Albert Herring* (Surrey Opera); *A Night at the Opera* (London Palladium and UK tour). Simon is one of the Jerwood Young Designers for 2013. www.simonkenny.co.uk

Amelia Lowdell – Carla

Theatre credits include: *Medea* (Headlong Tour); *Oxford Street*, *Breath Boom*, *Choices '98*, *Yard Gal* (all at the Royal Court, the latter of which transferred Off Broadway, New York); *Not Black and White* (Tricycle Theatre); *The Frontline* (Shakespeare's Globe); *A Bitter Herb* (Bristol Old Vic); *Great Expectations* (Manchester Royal Exchange). Film credits include: *Beginner's Luck, Essex Boys, Elephant Juice.* Television credits include: *Stepping Up, Case Sensitive, Injustice, The Shadow Line, The Bill, Casualty, Holby City, Silent Witness, Second Quest, Murder in Mind, Peak Practice, Every Woman Knows a Secret, The Vice.*

Tom Mills – Sound

Previous credits for the Gate include: *Wittenberg, Electra, Breathing Irregular, The Kreutzer Sonata, Unbroken.* Other theatre credits include: *Titus Andronicus, Ahasverus* (RSC); *Benefactors, The Way of the World* (Sheffield Crucible); *Huis Clos* (Donmar); *A Time To Reap, Wanderlust* (Royal Court); *Cesario, Prince of Denmark, The Eternal Not* (National); *Medea, Boys, A Midsummer Night's Dream, Edward Gant's Amazing Feats of Loneliness* (Headlong); *The Alchemist* (Liverpool Everyman); *The Dark at the Top of the Stairs* (Coventry Belgrade); *Great Expectations, Moonlight and Magnolias* (Watermill); *Bottleneck, Clockwork, Dusk Rings a Bell, Moscow Live* (Hightide); *Pericles, Macbeth* (Regent's Park Open Air Theatre); *The Boy Who Fell Into A Book, Utopia, Realism, Mongrel Island* (Soho); *Cinderella, Aladdin, Dick Whittington and his Cat* (Lyric); *Oliver Twist, Grimm Brother's Circus, The Jungle Book, Metropolis* (The Egg, Bath); *Elektra* (Young Vic); *Ditch* (Old Vic Tunnels) *Lidless* (Trafalgar Studios); *The Littlest Quirky* (Theatre Centre); *Rockpool* (Inspector Sands); *The Comedy of Errors* (Marlowe Society, Cambridge). Film credits include: *Funday, All In Good Time.*

Radio credits include: *The Afghan and the Penguin.*

Katy Munroe Farlie – Deputy Stage Manager

Katy graduated from the University of Hull in 2010 with a Degree in Theatre and Performance. From there she became the resident Production Manager for the New End Theatre until August 2011. Previous credits for the Gate include: *The Trojan Women.* Other theatre credits include: *Zelda, Barbershopera* (Trafagar Studios 2); *The Illusion, The Hairy Ape, Shivered* (Southwark Playhouse); *Twelfth Night* (Minack Theatre); *Herding Cats* (Hampstead Downstairs); *Blue Surge* (Finborough); *Bunny* (Soho Theatre Upstairs); *Mr Happiness and The Water Engine* (Old Vic Tunnels).

Bruce Norris – Writer

Bruce Norris is the author of the play *Clybourne Park,* which premiered in 2010 at Playwrights Horizons and in 2011-12 received the Pulitzer Prize for Drama, as well as the Olivier, Evening Standard, and Tony Awards for productions at the Royal Court, London, the West End and on Broadway. Other plays include *A Parallelogram, The Unmentionables, The Pain and the Itch, We All Went Down to Amsterdam,* and *The Infidel,* all of which premiered at Steppenwolf Theatre, Chicago. Two new plays, *The Low Road* and *Domesticated*, will premiere later this year at the Royal Court Theatre and Lincoln Centre Theatre (New York), respectively.

Dan Saggars – Production Electrician

Theatre credits include: *Romeo and Juliet/Spring Awakening* (Tour, Icarus Theatre Collective); *Mother Goose* (Millfield Arts Centre); *The Upstairs Room* (King's Head Theatre, Islington); *The Scarlet Pimpernel* (Wyllyott's Theatre, Potters Bar); *The Magic Flute, Katya* and *Gotterdamerung* (Longborough Festival Opera); *Little Foot* (Trestle Arts Base and Royal and Derngate, Northampton); *The Lonely One* (Little Angel Theatre); *Phaedra's Love* (The Arcola, Dalston); *The Story Project 3: Prayers, Promises and Platforms* (Southwark Playhouse).

Kate Schofield – Company Stage Manager

Kate trained at LAMDA. Previous credits for the Gate include: *Sunset Baby, The Prophet, The Measles, Franziska, Herakles*. Other theatre credits include: *Jack & The Beanstalk* (PHA Chesterfield Pomegranate); *Missing* (Gecko at Dance East, Ipswich); *His Teeth* (Only Connect); *Cinderella* (The Lighthouse Theatre); *The Comedy of Errors, The Importance of Being Earnest* (Oxford Shakespeare Company & regional outdoor tour); *Blackbirds* (London Bubble - Dilston Grove); *The Sirens of Titan* (London Bubble - outdoor tour); *The Southwark Mysteries* (Southwark Cathedral); *Anansi: An African Fairytale* (Southwark Playhouse).

John Tucker – Dialect Coach

John is Voice Tutor at RADA, a member of the teaching faculty at BADA, and runs a private voice studio in London (www.john-tucker.com). John is also Voice Associate at HighTide Festival Theatre. Previous credits for the Gate include: *The Prophet, Electra, How to Be Another Woman*. Other work as a voice coach includes: *A Midsummer Night's Dream* (Headlong); *Aristo* (Chichester Festival Theatre); *Bloody Poetry* (RADA); *Ditch* (Old Vic Tunnels); *Mother Courage* (English Touring Theatre); *Shallow Slumbers* (Soho Theatre); *Stovepipe* (National Theatre). Credits for TV include: *Classical Star* (BBC).

Trevor White – Purdy

Theatre credits include: *Long Day's Journey Into Night* (Apollo); *On the Record* (Arcola); *Twisted Tales* (Lyric Hammersmith); *Red Bud, Aunt Dan and Lemon* (Royal Court); *Macbeth* (Regent's Park); *Enron* (Chichester/ Royal Court/West End); *Lucky You* (Assembly Rooms); Coriolanus (RSC); *On the Piste* (Birmingham Rep); *House* (Finborough); *Double Indemnity, Polygraph* (Nottingham Playhouse); *Problem Child* (New End). Film credits include: *The Dark Knight Rises, World War Z, The Whistleblower, Genova, The Dark Knight: Gotham Tonight, Echelon Conspiracy, Mindhunters, Die Another Day, Hellraiser: Hellseeker.* Television credits include: *Hunted, Episodes, Downton Abbey, Foyle's War, Moonshot, Bonekickers, House of Saddam, Judge John Deed, The Path to 9/11, The Line of Beauty, Millennium.*

Jerwood Young Designers

***Purple Heart* Designer: Simon Kenny**

Since 2001 Jerwood Young Designers has given outstanding young designers the opportunity to work on productions in the versatile space of the Gate Theatre in Notting Hill.

The Gate has long had a reputation as having one of the most versatile studio spaces in London, perfect for young designers to explore theatrical possibilities. They also have the chance to work with some of the finest directors and writers working in theatre, an experience which is invaluable in establishing reputation and contacts.

The support that the Jerwood Young Designers scheme provides in both nurturing talent and offering the opportunity of practical experience has been instrumental in launching the careers of some of the country's most exciting theatrical designers.

www.jerwoodcharitablefoundation.org

GATE
THEATRE NOTTING HILL

"Queue, cajole or fight to get into this theatre" - *The Sunday Times*

The Gate is the UK's only small-scale theatre dedicated to producing a repertoire with a wholly international focus, meaning it occupies a unique position within Britain's diverse theatrical landscape. With an average audience capacity of 70, the Gate continues to challenge and inspire artists, making it famous for being one of London's most flexible and transformable theatre spaces.

For over 30 years, the Gate has been a powerhouse in British theatre, serving as a unique engine-room for talent. From directors at the early stages of their careers to exceptional actors, writers and designers all eager to create innovative and inspiring work, the Gate has always been a home for the spirited and anarchic souls of British theatre.

As the Gate's newest Artistic Director, Christopher Haydon continues the Gate's tradition of creating first-class and original theatre.

The Gate Theatre Company is a company limited by guarantee.
Registered in England & Wales No. 1495543 | Charity No. 280278
Registered address: 11 Pembridge Road, Above the Prince Albert Pub, London, W11 3HQ

Supported using public funding by
ARTS COUNCIL ENGLAND

GATE
THEATRE NOTTING HILL

Support the Gate

At the Gate, we want to keep taking artistic risks. We want to remain affordable for all. We want to encourage discussion and debate about the global issues that affect all our lives. We want to continue to be a place of possibilities, for you, and for emerging artists ready to take the leap. In order to take these risks and be the best we can be, we need your help.

Each year, to maintain our programming and achieve our aspirations, the Gate needs to raise a third of its income through private fundraising, from supporters like you. This year, that figure is £220,000.

We know it is a big ask, but at the Gate we believe you can see the incredible difference every penny you give makes, as soon as you walk through our doors. We look to you to guard the Gate – to act as ambassadors of our mission, and to donate towards our work. Your support means we can keep telling these challenging stories, in an intimate space, on an epic scale. At the Gate, the show might last an hour or two – the experience stays with you.

For more information on the Gate's work and how to support it, including our annual membership scheme and the range of benefits we are thrilled to offer to say thank you for your support, please visit www.gatetheatre.co.uk or contact Camilla Jackson on 020 7229 5387 or camilla@gatetheatre.co.uk.

The Gate would like to thank the following for their continued generous support:

Gate Guardians Katrina & Chris Barter, Miles Morland, Jon & NoraLee Sedmak, Anda & Bill Winters.
Gate Keepers Anonymous, Briony & Simon Bax, Eva Boenders & Scott Stevens, Vanessa Branson, Lauren Clancy, Charles Cormick & Steven Wheeler, Robert Devereux, Cory Edelman, Alexandra Emmerson, Leslie Feeney, Nick Ferguson, Joachim Fleury, Marianne Hinton, Robbi D. Holman, Linda & David Lakhdhir, Tony Mackintosh, Kate Maltby, David Pike, E & M Plantevin, Pascale Revert & Peter Wheeler, David & Susie Sainsbury, Faith Savage & Michael Gollner, Judith Scott, The Ulrich Family
Gate Lovers Anonymous, Rupert Christiansen, Susan Gibson & Mark Bergman, Jan & Richard Grandison, Kate Grimond, Stephen & Jennifer Harper, Sarah Havens & Gregg Sando, Mr & Mrs Michael Kelly, Brian & Janet King, Bill & Stephanie Knight, James & Anne-Marie Mackay, Keith & Alessandra Newman, Midge & Simon Palley, Herschel & Peggy Post, Paddy & Jacky Sellers.
Purple Heart Syndicate Supporters David Pike, Jon & NoraLee Sedmak. Special thanks to Jenny Hall.
Trusts & Foundations Arts Council England, Jerwood Charitable Foundation, OAK Foundation, Royal Borough of Kensington & Chelsea, Unity Theatre Trust. Artist in Residence at the Gate Theatre supported by Chelsea Arts Club Trust.

JERWOOD **CHARITABLE** FOUNDATION

PURPLE HEART

Bruce Norris

Author's Note

Purple Heart is a play I wrote in a period of my life that now seems – psychologically, if not chronologically – very distant to me. It was a period in which my personal life was in upheaval and also, significantly, not terribly long after September 11th, 2001, when the US was preparing to invade the nation of Iraq on the false pretext that they posed a threat to us. The real threat, as it would turn out, was from inside, a product of our collective paranoia and fear and desire for vengeance.

We performed the play in the summer of 2002 at Steppenwolf Theatre in Chicago – on the *large* stage, meaning it was very much a milestone in my so-called writing career – and then a year later we took the same production to the Galway Festival in Ireland. So, in addition to having positive associations with the play, personally, it was also the first time citizens of *another country* were listening to something I'd written. The tour was highly disorganised and we had roughly twelve hours to load the set into the theatre in Galway, undergo technical rehearsals, and then open to an Irish audience. The director and I stayed up all night painting the set and when we finally opened we collapsed from exhaustion.

It's always tricky to recall the exact state of mind you were in a decade ago. Suffice it to say that during that time I had developed terrible doubts about the nature of love and kindness (and if the two are mutually exclusive), as well about the problematic imperial role played by the US in the larger world. And how the desire to hurt and the desire to help often become difficult to distinguish.

B.N.
January 2013

Purple Heart was first produced by Steppenwolf Theatre
Company (artistic director, Martha Lavey) on 5 July, 2002,
with the following cast:

THOR	Nathan Kiley
CARLA	Laurie Metcalf
GRACE	Rosemary Prinz
PURDY	Christopher Evan Welch

Director	Anna D. Shapiro
Set Designer	Daniel P. Ostling
Costume Designer	James Schuette
Lighting Designer	James F. Ingalls
Sound Designers	Rob Milburn and Michael Bodeen
Stage Manager	Laura D. Glenna

Characters

THOR
GRACE
CARLA
PURDY

THOR *is twelve. He has long hair and wears tinted*
'aviator'-style glasses.

GRACE *is sixty-five and wears a hearing aid.*

CARLA *is in her thirties.*

PURDY *is in his twenties. He wears a corporal's uniform. He is*
a large man with short hair and glasses and a polite manner.

This is a medium-sized city in the Midwest. The set is the living
room of Carla and Thor's home, with exits to a kitchen and
dining room, one to the front door, and another to a hallway off
of which other rooms are located. We can see down the hallway,
but the front door is not visible. The house was built in the late
fifties but has been decorated (tastefully, not tacky) in the
modern way, i.e. shag rugs, contemporary lighting fixtures and
so forth.

There should be no music of any kind in the play except where
indicated.

The time is late October, 1972.

This text went to press before the end of rehearsals and so may
differ slightly from the play as performed.

ACT ONE

Six p.m., central daylight time. The room is almost totally dark.
THOR *enters from the hallway. He turns on a lamp,*
illuminating CARLA, *who is asleep on the sofa. She wears a*
bathrobe over her clothes. THOR *studies her briefly, then*
makes a circuit around the room turning on other lights.
CARLA *remains asleep.*

He goes to the stereo and picks up a record. He places it on the
turntable, then leaves the room. An aggressive rock song begins
to play at a very high volume. CARLA *remains asleep.* THOR
re-enters with a stepladder. He places it near a wall and climbs
up. He removes a clock from the wall and opens its back.

GRACE *enters from the front hallway. She wears a coat and*
scarf and carries her purse.

GRACE. Thor?

    He does not respond. GRACE *patiently repeats herself.*

    Thor? Thor? Thor? Thor?

    She takes the needle off the record.

    Thor.

    He still does not respond.

    I'm speaking to you, Thor.

THOR. I know.

GRACE. I'd like you to answer me when I speak to you.

THOR. I'm answering.

GRACE *(re: the clock)*. What are you doing with that?

THOR. Changing the time.

GRACE. Did you ask before doing that?

THOR. No.

GRACE. Is there something wrong with it?

THOR. No.

GRACE. Maybe we should leave it the way it is.

THOR. Spring forward fall back.

GRACE. Oh I see.

THOR. I'm doing them all.

GRACE. I see now. Well. Thank you, then. And you know what you're doing?

THOR. It is oh so challenging.

GRACE. It *is* an expensive clock, Thor.

THOR (*innocently*). Did you pay for it?

GRACE. I think we ought to ask your mother before we do something like that.

THOR (*to* CARLA). Mom, can I set the clock back?

CARLA *does not stir.*

She doesn't mind.

GRACE. I don't trust that ladder. Is that ladder safe?

THOR. I don't know.

GRACE. Let's avoid having an accident.

GRACE *exits down the hallway.* THOR *replaces the clock on the wall and descends the ladder. He sits next to* CARLA.

THOR. She's back.

She does not stir. THOR *continues patiently.*

Mom. Mom. Mom. Mom.

He takes her arm and removes her wristwatch. He resets the time, then replaces it on her wrist.

Mom. Mom. Mom.

He pinches her nose. She pulls her head away but does not open her eyes.

CARLA. Don't.

THOR. She's back.

CARLA. Don't do that to me.

THOR. You said wake you up when she got back.

CARLA. I'm awake.

THOR. Now you are.

CARLA. Don't pinch my nose.

THOR. Get up.

CARLA. I'm up.

THOR. No you're not.

CARLA. Go away.

THOR. Lazy ass.

CARLA. Go away.

THOR. Lazy ass.

CARLA. Watch it.

THOR. Lazy fucking ass.

CARLA. You're about to get your ass *whipped*.

THOR. I'm scared.

CARLA. Keep it up.

THOR. Like to see you try.

CARLA. Keep it up.

THOR. Have to get off your ass first.

CARLA. Keep it up.

THOR. Your lazy ass.

CARLA. Toilet mouth.

THOR. Ass face.

CARLA. I'm not going to speak to you.

THOR. What a tragedy.

CARLA. I'm not going to speak to a toilet mouth.

THOR. Oh no. Not speak? Please. Anything but that.

A long pause.

Aaah. Peace and quiet. Peace at last.

He grows restless.

Did I get my package?

CARLA *does nothing.* THOR *kicks her.*

Answer me. Where is it? Answer me. Cut it out. Answer me.

CARLA *sticks out her tongue.*

God you're ugly. Old and lazy and ugly. Answer me. Did it come? Stop it.

CARLA *wiggles her tongue.*

You're disgusting. You look disgusting when you do that. Stop it. Answer me. I hate you. Lazy whore.

CARLA *opens her eyes and sits up.*

CARLA. *Hey.*

THOR. *What?*

CARLA. *Watch what you say to me, you little piece of shit.*

THOR. *So try answering me for a change.*

CARLA. *I did answer you but you better watch your mouth.*

THOR. *No you didn't.*

CARLA. *And don't do things to me while I'm asleep.*

THOR. *You said to wake you up.*

Pause.

CARLA. How long has she been back?

THOR. Couple of minutes. Where is it?

CARLA. Where is what?

THOR. My package. I asked you ten times.

CARLA. I don't know.

THOR. Why is it taking so long?

CARLA. I don't know.

THOR. Fucking rip-off.

CARLA. It'll come.

THOR. When?

CARLA. I don't know.

THOR. Never.

CARLA. Maybe tomorrow.

THOR. Maybe never.

CARLA. Few more days.

THOR. I better get some money back.

> THOR *reaches in his pocket and pulls out a 'finger guillotine' from a novelty shop.*

> Put your finger in here.

CARLA. No.

THOR. Do it.

CARLA. I don't want to.

THOR. Do it.

CARLA. No.

THOR. Do it.

CARLA. No.

THOR. *Yes.*

CARLA. *I don't want to.*

THOR. You have to.

CARLA. I'm not going to do it.

> THOR *finds a pencil and inserts it in the guillotine. He chops it in half. Then he takes a trick knife and a tube of fake blood out of his pocket. He holds the knife to his throat.*

THOR. Look.

CARLA. No.

THOR. I'm gonna stab myself.

CARLA. I don't like it.

THOR. Look. You *baby.*

CARLA. All right, all right.

> *He pushes the knife into his throat and squeezes the fake blood on his neck.*

> *Very* funny.

THOR. I'm bleeding.

CARLA. Don't get that on the sofa.

THOR. I'm dying.

CARLA. I don't want that blood on the sofa.

THOR. It washes out.

CARLA. Well, I don't *want* to wash it out.

> *He wipes the blood off of his neck.*

THOR. What happened to Chet and Gibby?

CARLA. How should I know?

THOR. They never come over.

CARLA. They have their own things to do.

THOR. Like what?

CARLA. I don't know and frankly I don't care.

THOR. Call them.

CARLA. They go to *college*, Thor.

THOR. So?

CARLA. So the whole world doesn't revolve around you.

THOR. Yes it does.

CARLA. They're *your* friends.

THOR. They like *you*.

CARLA. You call them.

THOR. Where do I get the number?

CARLA. Look in the phone book.

THOR. I don't know where it is.

CARLA. Well, that's *your* problem.

Pause. THOR *takes something out of his pocket.*

THOR. Oh no. I feel sick.

CARLA. Don't do that.

THOR. I'm gonna puke.

CARLA. I've seen it.

THOR. Oh no. Here it comes. Look. Look. You're not looking.

CARLA. All right. I'm looking.

THOR. Oh no. Oh no.

He makes a gagging noise and drops a plastic vomit on the coffee table.

Ahhh. That's better.

CARLA. Very good.

THOR. Looks real.

CARLA. Very realistic.

GRACE *enters, carrying a laundry basket. At the sound of her voice,* THOR *picks up the vomit and starts out of the room.*

GRACE. Yoo-hoo? Here I am. So, are you awake then, dear?

CARLA. I'm awake.

GRACE. Thor?

THOR (*stopping*). What?

GRACE. Where are you going?

THOR. My room.

GRACE. Have you been inside all day?

THOR. Mostly.

GRACE. Maybe you'd like to go *outside* on the weekends.

THOR. What for?

GRACE. Some fresh air.

THOR. My window is open.

GRACE. Or a little exercise. Where's your football?

THOR. There's no air in it.

GRACE. Why don't you see if you can find the pump?

THOR. Then what?

GRACE. Tomorrow you could play with it.

THOR. By myself?

GRACE. With one of your friends.

THOR *stares at her for a moment, then walks out of the room.*

(*To* THOR, *as he leaves*.) I hope you're going to put this ladder away. (*To* CARLA.) That ladder is a crisis in the making.

CARLA *does not respond.*

I don't suppose you had a chance to go to the market.

CARLA. I wasn't feeling very well.

GRACE. Yes.

CARLA. Sorry.

GRACE. But you're feeling better now.

CARLA. A little better.

GRACE. You needed the rest. It's your stomach again?

CARLA. Mm-hmm.

GRACE. Did you find the Milk of Magnesia?

CARLA. No.

GRACE. Did you look next to my bed?

CARLA. Not really.

GRACE. Why don't I get it for you?

CARLA. I'm better now.

GRACE. I'm happy to do it.

CARLA. I'm fine.

GRACE. All right then. (*Beat.*) I'm glad you're feeling better.

CARLA. Thanks.

   Pause.

GRACE. Unfortunately, we are still out of milk.

CARLA. Oh. You didn't stop, then?

GRACE. Well, you had suggested that *you* would.

CARLA. I can still go.

GRACE. If I had known that you weren't going I would have been happy to go. But I was under the impression that you had gone. The Pastor drove me right past the market.

CARLA. Okay.

GRACE. Right past without even slowing down. And there's very little butter.

CARLA. I'll put on some clothes and go.

GRACE. The butter isn't important. I can cook with the Crisco oil.

CARLA. Just give me a couple of minutes.

GRACE. But I do prefer milk for my coffee. (*Laughs*.) If it's between that and Crisco oil.

CARLA. No, I know.

GRACE. And I suppose we don't really need a green salad.

CARLA. There's lettuce.

GRACE. Yes.

CARLA. Look in the crisper.

GRACE. I did.

CARLA. There's a whole head of lettuce in there.

GRACE. Well, it seems to have rather wilted.

   Pause.

CARLA. Give me three minutes and I'll go.

GRACE. Well, the market's *closed*, dear.

CARLA (*looks at her watch*). They close at six.

GRACE. It's six-thirty.

CARLA. It's *five*-thirty.

GRACE. No.

CARLA. Look at the clock.

GRACE. Thor changed the clock.

CARLA. Why?

GRACE. And I suppose he must have changed your wristwatch as well.

CARLA. *It's five-thirty.*

GRACE. Tomorrow at this time it will be five-thirty, *standard* time. Right now it is actually six-thirty *daylight* time.

CARLA. Oh.

GRACE. He did us a little favour before we go to sleep.

CARLA. Oh.

GRACE. So I think we'd best abandon our plans concerning the market.

CARLA. Well. In that case.

GRACE. Doesn't matter to me. I'm happy to have a ham sandwich. There's still a good amount of that ham left. I love a nice ham sandwich and a glass of... (*Remembering.*) well, I don't suppose it has to be milk.

CARLA. I'll go first thing tomorrow.

GRACE. Would you care for a ham sandwich?

CARLA. I'm not hungry.

GRACE. Well, I believe *I* will. That ham that Mrs Lacy brought over is *very* tasty, I have to say. Certainly no more difficult to make two. But I won't press. Thor, however, would probably prefer some sort of hot dish. We had that noodle casserole from the Osterbergs, but I believe it's gone bad.

CARLA. I'm sorry I didn't go, Grace. I had every intention of going. I'm sorry.

GRACE. No apology necessary. Oh yes. Let's see. The Pastor wanted to know if tomorrow at two would be a good time.

CARLA. Tomorrow?

GRACE. Or did you have plans?

CARLA. Not exactly.

GRACE. What are your plans?

CARLA. I don't have plans.

GRACE. Don't change them if you have them.

CARLA. I don't have them.

GRACE. So two is all right then?

CARLA. What does he want to talk about?

GRACE. He's interested in how you are doing.

CARLA. I spoke to him on the phone.

GRACE. Briefly.

CARLA. I told him I was fine.

GRACE. Wouldn't a visit be that much more pleasant?

CARLA. What time tomorrow?

GRACE. After the second service.

CARLA. I – I – I – I – I don't –

GRACE. That way you'll be able to speak freely.

CARLA. I'm supposed to speak *freely*?

GRACE. I don't know.

CARLA. How *freely* does he want me to speak?

GRACE. I don't know.

CARLA. Cuz I'll be happy to speak freely. If that's what he – In fact, don't just bring the Pastor. There's gotta be one or two people in the neighborhood that haven't stopped by. Bring 'em along. Bring the congregation. We'll do it in shifts.

GRACE. It is traditional. For the clergy to participate.

CARLA. In my life?

GRACE. In the grieving process.

Beat.

CARLA. Let me see how I feel.

GRACE. Well, he is *planning* to come at two.

CARLA. So asking me was just a *formality*.

GRACE. I'll call him now if you'd rather reschedule.

CARLA. No.

GRACE. But that is his *plan*.

Silence for a few moments.

CARLA. Two is fine.

GRACE. I'll see what we have to make a hot dish.

CARLA. *What* time is it?

GRACE. It's six-thirty.

CARLA. That clock is crooked.

No one moves.

GRACE. Did the doctor say anything?

CARLA. Well. You know. I'm run-down. The hospital didn't catch the anaemia, so that's worse. And on top of that the upset stomach. Probably some kind of virus, he said, some kind of I don't know some kind of twenty-four-hour kind of thing. That sort of thing. You know. That *kind* of thing. He wasn't very specific.

GRACE. He didn't say anything else?

CARLA. Like what?

GRACE. I don't know.

CARLA. What kind of thing?

GRACE. That's what I'm asking *you*.

CARLA. What else should he say?

GRACE. Something more specific.

CARLA. I just told you what he said.

GRACE. All right.

CARLA. I don't understand what you're asking.

GRACE. He didn't give you anything?

CARLA. What would he give me?

GRACE. He didn't *prescribe* anything.

CARLA. No.

GRACE. All right. I will offer the Milk of Magnesia once again.

CARLA. No thanks.

GRACE. Well. The offer stands.

   Pause.

CARLA. I was just *resting*, Grace. I just needed to *rest*.

GRACE. I know.

CARLA. It's not – I mean – I haven't been *feeling* well and –
   and – and – (*Continues.*)

GRACE (*overlapping*). I understand that.

CARLA. – and just because I might need to *rest* from time to
   time I don't see anything particularly *sinister* in that –
   (*Continues.*)

GRACE (*overlapping*). I didn't say that there was.

CARLA. – I just need to *rest* and yes, I know you *say* that, but
   still there are these – these – these – these little *silences*
   because you know being sick is not – especially given the
   circumstances – (*Continues.*)

GRACE (*overlapping*). I fully understand.

CARLA. – what I'm saying is being sick is not a *crime*, it's not
   evidence of some personal *failure* or – or – or – I mean Jesus
   Christ people get sick and I'm sorry if I happen to be one of
   those people. You've never been sick a day in your life, of
   course, you would never do that but God forbid you ever *do*
   I mean God forbid because what would that say about *you,*
   you know? I'd hate to think.

   Pause.

GRACE. No need to swear, dear.

CARLA. Sorry.

GRACE. So many other ways to express oneself.

CARLA. Right.

GRACE. Your mind is too original for that.

Pause.

Well, let's see. My day was rather interesting. Esther and I
had lunch at The Pantry with Esther's friend Joanne
Nierengarten. It turns out that Joanne's husband had
oesophageal cancer. Seems they had to remove a substantial
amount of his oesophagus and refashion the rest out of the
existing stomach tissue, which just sounds like a hideous
procedure. There's one thing to be grateful for: we have our
health. Never overlook the blessing of good health. (*Beat*.)
Did you know that The Pantry has taken the Neptune Salad
off of the lunch menu? I told the girl I had ordered that salad
for the last twenty-five years and it simply baffled me that
they would make such an arbitrary decision. She said we can
make it for you special but I said that was hardly the point
the point was if a business has succeeded by offering a
satisfying product then oughtn't it behoove the business to
continue to offer that product as long as the customer shows
enthusiasm for it? Doesn't seem like good business. Doesn't
make sense to me but then maybe I have become irrelevant.
Maybe that is the lesson I'm to learn: the lesson of my own
irrelevance. Perhaps that's it. My obsolescence.

Pause.

But they made the salad for me and it was tasty. As it always
has been. And we have our health.

Pause.

Then when I got back to the office there was quite a
controversy as two men from the contractors had arrived to
install the new commode next to the vestry. Now, the Pastor
had been absolutely clear that the model he had requested
was a silent-flush model but these two gentlemen were in

adamant disagreement. So I produced the paperwork and said, gentlemen, you have been confronted with the evidence of your mistake and I will not allow you to compound it by proceeding. And with the help of the custodian, I blocked their way. (*With a shake of the head.*) The vulgarity of the language. As he drove me home the Pastor said thank you, Grace, another crisis narrowly averted.

Pause.

But I do hope they put that salad back on the menu.

Pause.

Well, perhaps I'll see about making that sandwich.

GRACE *does not move*.

(*Simply.*) Have you been drinking today, dear?

CARLA. No. I haven't.

GRACE. You haven't.

CARLA. But I appreciate you asking.

GRACE. I had hoped we were past that.

CARLA. We are.

GRACE. Since the hospital.

CARLA. We're past it, Grace.

GRACE. All right then.

CARLA. All right then.

GRACE. You know when Gene died I felt for quite some time that I wouldn't be able to go on. I did. Yet here I am. I know you don't think so right now but you will feel better some day. I think I have enough experience to say this.

Pause.

So perhaps those two young men were here today.

CARLA. What two young men?

GRACE. I can't remember their *names*.

CARLA. Chet and Gibby?

GRACE. From Fourth of July.

CARLA. Why would you think they were here?

GRACE. I don't think I was ever introduced.

CARLA. What would they be doing here?

GRACE. I don't know, dear. You're the one who's friendly with them.

CARLA. They're friends of Thor's.

GRACE. In a sense.

CARLA. They happen to like Thor.

GRACE. And they like you as well.

Pause.

CARLA. Grace.

GRACE. I was an attractive woman at one time.

CARLA. Okay, Grace.

GRACE. I know that may be difficult to picture. But I don't want you to think that I don't understand what it is like. Because I *do* understand.

CARLA. Thor met them at the *pool*. They work at the *pool*.

GRACE. Yes, it's nice for him to make some friends.

CARLA. They taught him how to do a backflip.

GRACE. But if I remember correctly the day that they were here before, Thor spent the evening watching television with me while they smoked and drank outside on the patio with you.

CARLA. Grace.

GRACE. And I'm not entirely sure what benefit Thor derived from that. In fact, as I recall, they were here long after Thor went to sleep.

CARLA. We… *talked*. I – I – I honestly don't know why I'm having to – I liked *talking* to them, we were… I don't know why I am *justifying* having *talked* to a couple of – (*Continues*.)

GRACE (*overlapping*). I'm simply trying to understand.

CARLA. – I mean who am I going to *talk* to, Grace? Who do you expect me to talk to? In the course of a day. Who do I talk to? I'm asking you. Honestly. Who? Honestly. You tell me.

GRACE. *We're* talking, aren't we?

Pause.

CARLA. In answer to your question, no. They were not here today.

GRACE. Well. I thought I would ask.

CARLA. Okay.

GRACE. Because I found this in your laundry hamper.

She pulls a vodka bottle out of the basket.

And so I made that assumption.

Beat.

CARLA. *I'm* going to do the laundry.

GRACE. Well, we also seem to be out of *detergent*.

CARLA. No we're not.

GRACE. I believe we are.

CARLA. There's a brand-new box.

GRACE. I didn't see one.

CARLA. Right on top of the machine.

GRACE. I don't think so, but –

CARLA. Did you *look*? You must not have looked.

GRACE. I did, but –

CARLA. Follow me. I'll show you exactly where it is.

GRACE. I believe you.

CARLA. But you're implying that I forgot to get detergent.

GRACE. I didn't say that.

CARLA. And the fact of the matter is that I *did*.

GRACE. All right then. But –

CARLA. It's a bright-orange box. It's impossible to miss it.

GRACE. But since your young men drank *beer* that night, rather than liquor, the beer that has been sitting all this time in our refrigerator, and since this bottle is half-empty, I thought you might know where it came from.

Pause.

CARLA. Wouldn't it be nicer to say it's half-*full*?

GRACE. Have you been drinking today?

THOR *has silently appeared.*

THOR. It's mine.

CARLA. Go away.

GRACE. This is a private conversation, Thor.

THOR. I drank it.

CARLA. Don't.

GRACE. It's not polite to eavesdrop on a private conversation.

THOR. I just walked in and you were talking.

GRACE. All right.

THOR. Why is it private?

GRACE. We can talk about that later.

THOR. I have to talk to Mom.

GRACE. What about?

THOR. It's private.

GRACE. After we're done, then.

THOR. When will that be?

CARLA. Get your little ass out of here.

GRACE. Oh, no. Oh no, dear. No. Really. Dear. Not the language.

THOR. Can I have my vodka?

Pause.

GRACE (*to* THOR). If it's yours, where did you get it?

THOR. Liquor store.

GRACE. I see. And you drank half of this bottle?

THOR. Yep.

GRACE. And when was this?

THOR. Today.

GRACE. Today.

THOR. Yeah.

GRACE. You went to the liquor store today.

THOR. Yeah.

GRACE. While your mother was here.

THOR. She was asleep.

A high-pitched whining sound begins. THOR *and* CARLA *cover their ears.* GRACE *is oblivious.*

GRACE. What liquor store was this?

CARLA. Grace?

GRACE. Because tomorrow you and I can go back there and talk to the proprietor.

CARLA. *Grace.*

GRACE. And we can ask him why he would sell – *what*?

CARLA. Batteries, Grace.

GRACE. You need to *enunciate*, dear.

THOR. *Batteries. Batteries. Batteries.* – (*Continues.*)

CARLA (*overlapping* THOR). *The batteries.*

GRACE (*overlapping* THOR). I don't know what that is. I've never heard of a *paddery*.

THOR. – *Turn it down turn it down turn it down turn it down* – (*Continues.*)

CARLA (*overlapping*). *Batteries, Grace. The batteries in the thing.* (*Points to her ear.*)

THOR. – *turn it down turn it down turn it down turn it down.*

GRACE. Thor. We don't need to sh– Oh. I see.

She adjusts the volume. The whistling stops.

If you feel compelled to *shout* you can go outside.

The doorbell rings. No one moves. CARLA *sits. Then* GRACE *sits. Then* THOR. *It rings again.* THOR *goes to answer it. Silence. After twenty seconds or so, he returns.*

THOR (*to* CARLA). A guy wants to talk to you.

CARLA (*with disgust*). What *guy*?

THOR. I don't know.

GRACE (*to* CARLA). Were you expecting someone?

CARLA. Who would I be expecting?

GRACE (*to* THOR). What is his name?

THOR. I don't know.

GRACE. Did you ask?

THOR. No.

GRACE. Did he say what he wanted?

THOR. To see Mom.

GRACE. Why, I mean?

CARLA. Why do you *think*?

THOR. No.

GRACE. He didn't say?

CARLA. To *console* me.

GRACE. What sort of man?

CARLA. To bring me another *casserole*.

THOR (*to* GRACE). An army guy.

CARLA. Say I'm sick.

> THOR *goes. A pause, then:*

GRACE. I would *hope*, *w*ere the shoe on the other foot, and *you* had made the effort –

CARLA. On the *what*?

GRACE. I understand your irritation with *me*.

CARLA. What are you saying?

GRACE. Well. When someone goes out of their *way*.

CARLA. I'm in my *bathrobe*.

GRACE. You have a legitimate grievance with me. It's understandable.

CARLA. Grace. I – I – I – What is the *point* of that? Who uses words like *grievance*?

GRACE. It's not impolite to be *precise*.

CARLA. It's just – it's just – it's just – (*Continues*.)

CARLA – how did it become *my* responsibility to entertain total *strangers*?	GRACE. And if a person has gone out of their way to make you an offer of *kindness* –

CARLA. Samaritans. Yes. I know.

GRACE. – It could be – that is, it is *possible* that one might *benefit* from avoiding isolation.

CARLA. *Isolation?*

GRACE. It's possible.

CARLA. But how would I *know?* Lemme *try* some isolation and maybe we'll find out.

THOR *has re-entered.*

GRACE. Yes, Thor?

THOR. He says his name is Purdy.

CARLA. *Christ.*

THOR. Says it'll only take ten minutes.

CARLA *groans, rises and exits toward the hallway during the following.*

CARLA *(muttering to herself).* There was a *time*, ya know, a *time* when people could take a subtle *hint.* When you didn't have to *spell it out. (Publicly.)* Well, by all *means.* Bring him in. Bring 'em all in. Casserole for dinner *tonight*, Grace.

A door slams. She is gone.

GRACE. I'll make some coffee.

GRACE *goes into the kitchen.* THOR *exits. We hear a door close.* PURDY *enters.* THOR *follows.* PURDY *wears a corporal's uniform. His right hand is artificial.*

THOR. Did you bring a casserole?

PURDY. A what?

THOR. Casserole.

PURDY. No.

A pause. THOR *sits.* PURDY *sits.*

THOR. Do you want a beer?

PURDY. No thank you, son.

THOR. We have some.

PURDY. No thank you.

THOR. You want a Coke?

PURDY. No thanks.

THOR. I drink beer sometimes.

PURDY. Okay.

THOR. You don't like the way it tastes?

PURDY. Tastes fine.

THOR. So why don't you drink it?

PURDY. Personal reasons.

THOR. What about whiskey?

PURDY. No.

THOR. What about vodka?

PURDY. No.

THOR. What about Kahlua?

PURDY. No.

THOR. What about Andre's Cold Duck?

PURDY. No.

THOR. Are you religious?

PURDY. No.

Pause.

THOR. What about Harvey's Bristol Cream?

PURDY. I'll have some coffee. If you have some coffee.

THOR stands and goes into the kitchen. PURDY sits and stares for almost a full minute. THOR returns and sits.

THOR. My grandmother's making it.

PURDY. Okay.

THOR. She said about five minutes.

PURDY. Sounds good.

Pause.

THOR. What happened to your hand?

PURDY. Buried ordnance.

THOR. Blew your hand off.

PURDY. Mm-hm.

THOR. Is that a fake hand?

PURDY. Yep.

THOR. What's it made of?

PURDY. Fibreglass.

THOR. How does it stay on?

PURDY. Has a strap on it.

THOR. Leather strap.

PURDY. Uh-huh.

THOR. Where does the strap go?

PURDY. Around the forearm.

THOR. Why didn't you get one of those claws?

PURDY. Didn't like the way it looked.

THOR. But you could pick stuff up.

PURDY. I guess that's right.

Pause.

THOR. You want a magazine?

PURDY. No thanks.

Pause. THOR *takes out the finger guillotine.*

THOR. Put your finger in here.

PURDY. No thanks.

THOR. Why not?

PURDY. Just rather not.

THOR. Scared to.

PURDY. No.

THOR. Scared it'll chop your finger off.

PURDY. Nope.

THOR. So do it.

PURDY. I know how those work.

THOR. So?

PURDY. I'm not very interested in jokes and novelties.

THOR *puts the guillotine away.*

What grade you in?

THOR. Sixth.

PURDY. Make good grades?

THOR. Yeah.

PURDY. A's and B's?

THOR. Yeah.

PURDY. Not so hard, then.

THOR. Fuckin' easy.

PURDY. Okay.

Pause.

THOR. Do you know how to make a punji trap?

PURDY. No.

THOR. I want to know how deep a hole you have to dig.

PURDY. I don't know. Fairly deep, I suppose.

THOR. Do you have to make the spikes out of bamboo or could they just be wood spikes?

PURDY. Wood could probably do you just as well.

THOR. But it's not that hard to make.

PURDY. You may be right.

THOR. And then you shit on them.

PURDY. On the spikes.

THOR. For poison. So when you fall on the spikes you get poisoned by the shit.

PURDY. Hmm.

THOR. Think if you fell in. Like if you were standing over the hole shitting on the spikes and all of a sudden you were slipping and then you were like '*whoa*' and you fell in the hole with your pants down and died like that.

PURDY. I would imagine that the faeces is applied before the sticks are planted in the trap rather than deposited from overhead.

Pause. THOR *considers this.*

Mind checking on that coffee for me?

THOR *(top of his lungs).* IS THE COFFEE READY?

PURDY. How about if you *go* and check?

THOR *stands and goes. And once again he returns and sits.*

THOR. Not yet.

PURDY. Okay.

Pause.

THOR. Do you know the capital of Greenland?

PURDY. No.

THOR. Godthåb.

PURDY. Huh.

THOR. Do you know the capital of Burundi?

PURDY. No.

THOR. Bujumbura.

PURDY. Huh.

THOR. Do you know the capital of Kentucky?

PURDY. Frankfort.

THOR. Most people say Louisville.

PURDY. It's Frankfort.

Pause.

THOR. Did you ever fuck any whores?

PURDY. Does your mother know you use that kind of language?

THOR. She taught me this language.

PURDY. No. I didn't.

THOR. Suckee suckee five buckee. My friend Ricky Purzer has a cousin in the Marines and he says there's all these whores and they always say suckee suckee five buckee.

PURDY. Your mother must be a very special person.

THOR. Hey, G.I. Joe, me love you long time.

PURDY. A very unique person.

THOR. My friend Ricky's cousin saw Andy Williams do a show.

PURDY. Okay.

THOR. Did you see that show?

PURDY. No.

THOR. And Flip Wilson and Nancy Sinatra.

PURDY. Huh.

THOR. And Tiny Tim from *Laugh-In*.

Pause.

I think if you made a punji trap it'd have to be at least six feet
deep because if you weren't falling fast enough the spikes
wouldn't go in very far. This guy down the street Matt
Cressap? He has a Husqvarna and sometimes he takes the cap
off the gas tank and he puts his cigarette out in the gas tank but
the reason it doesn't blow up is because it's only the vapours
that blow up and if you do it really fast the vapours don't blow
up and it just goes out like pfffft and all the little kids are like
running away like *ahhh* 'cause they're so scared it's gonna
explode. (*Beat*.) I figured out how to make jelly gas. If you
take styrofoam? You know the kind that they have at like a
flower shop and you put it in gasoline it dissolves and turns
into jelly gas and you can light it and throw it and it explodes.
I made a flame-thrower too with a can of hairspray.

Pause. PURDY *nods*.

Did you ever eat dog meat?

PURDY. The *flesh* of a dog?

THOR. Yeah.

PURDY. No.

THOR. But people do.

PURDY. What people?

THOR. Where you were.

PURDY. It's possible.

THOR. All the time.

PURDY. I don't know.

THOR. They love it. Barbecued dog.

PURDY. Hm.

THOR. I would eat dog.

PURDY. Okay.

THOR. To stay alive. Think if you were starving.

PURDY. Sure.

THOR. You'd have to. People say they wouldn't but they all would if they had to.

PURDY. Maybe so.

THOR. You wouldn't have a choice. But people over there don't eat it because they have to. They like it. They do. It's their favourite thing.

PURDY. I wouldn't know.

THOR. Suckee suckee five buckee. (*Chinese accent.*) Ah-so. Me rike more dog meat, prease.

Pause.

You never saw that? People eating a dog?

PURDY. No.

THOR. Oh.

Pause.

PURDY. I did see a dog eat a *person.*

GRACE *enters with coffee, a slice of cake and a fork. At the sound of her voice,* THOR *starts to leave.*

GRACE. Yoo-hoo. Here we are then. Thor?

THOR (*stops*). What?

GRACE. Are you going to move that ladder?

THOR. I don't predict the future.

THOR *goes.*

GRACE (*to* PURDY). I don't trust that ladder. Well. Isn't this a treat? I always say there's nothing quite so nice as an unexpected guest. Always a treat.

PURDY. Thank you, ma'am.

GRACE. Lars had so many friends. I always knew that he was popular with his crowd but I have to say, Mr Birney, it has been a bit overwhelming to see just how true that was. Do you take sugar?

PURDY. Black, please.

GRACE. There's also a bit of cake. Do you like cake?

PURDY. Not for me.

GRACE. Do you know the Livelys? Marjorie Lively made it.

PURDY. No.

GRACE. Don and Marjorie Lively?

PURDY. No.

GRACE. I'm surprised. Well. You know, my *father* loved entertaining. He was *convivial*. My mother, on the other hand, was retiring by nature. But then, she was ill for much of her life. I would offer you milk but it seems we had a bit of miscommunication about the market. (*Realising.*) Oh dear. You did say *black* quite clearly, didn't you?

PURDY. Either way.

GRACE. The sweet one will be for me, then. The sweeter the better. (*Pouring.*) Here we go, then. Black as midnight, as Lars would say.

PURDY. It's *Purdy*.

GRACE. Beg pardon?

PURDY. *Purdy.* (*Points to his nametag.*) Rather than *Birney*.

GRACE (*re: her hearing aid*). Oh my gracious. Do you know, I spend a *king's ransom* on batteries for this device.

PURDY. It's all right.

GRACE. The world can get *cacophonous*. But as the world turns *up* its volume, nature has done me the favour of turning mine *down*.

PURDY. What did she suffer from?

GRACE. Whom?

PURDY. Your mother was ill, you said.

GRACE. Oh. She was born with her internal organs reversed.

Beat.

PURDY. Really?

GRACE. Yes.

PURDY. Is that right?

GRACE. Oh, yes.

PURDY. Reversed?

GRACE. Mm-hm.

PURDY. That's unusual.

GRACE. Extremely.

PURDY. This was a diagnosis?

GRACE. Oh, yes.

PURDY. Reversed left to right?

GRACE. Yes.

PURDY. Huh.

PURDY *thinks*.

Would that make a *difference*?

GRACE. Apparently it does. She was by no means convivial. When did you arrive home?

PURDY. Very recently.

GRACE. I don't know how you do it. The lack of routine. I couldn't. Lars was well suited, though. Never one to complain. Like my father. How long had you known each other?

PURDY. Known whom?

GRACE. You probably knew him as *Whitey*. Tow-headed as a boy, you know. Straw-coloured later on but somehow the name stuck.

PURDY. So *Lars* was also known as *Whitey*.

GRACE. Whitey Larsen. Although my daughter-in-law tells me that the name may have gained an unfortunate *racial* connotation.

PURDY. Whitey? Could be.

GRACE. How sad the way innocent things can get twisted. I have to tell you I don't envy young people. What a difficult time to be young. With the anger and the vulgarity and the controversy. It was very different for me. Back in *the dark ages*. My father would always say *if you can't say something nice, don't say anything at all* and of course I bristled at that back then but as time goes on the wisdom of that advice becomes more apparent.

PURDY. If you can't say something *nice*.

GRACE. Yes.

PURDY. Of course, that might lead to the occasional extended period of *silence*.

GRACE. I don't think silence is anything to be afraid of.

An extended period of silence. GRACE *grows afraid.* CARLA *enters, dressed with minimal care.*

(*Relieved.*) Oh. Well then. Here we are. Dear, this is Corporal *Purdy*. I believe I've got that right now, haven't I?

PURDY. Yes, ma'am. Hello.

GRACE. Want to make sure. Had a bit of silliness with the name. I'm still red in the face.

PURDY. Doesn't matter.

GRACE. My mind is like as old lawnmower. Takes a few *pulls* to get it started.

PURDY (*to* CARLA). I'm sorry. I should have called.

GRACE. Not at all.

PURDY. It being the dinner hour.

GRACE. On another occasion I would ask you to join us.

PURDY. No thank you.

GRACE. But on another occasion.

PURDY (*to* CARLA). I… understand you're not feeling well.

CARLA. I'm fine.

PURDY. Oh. All right.

CARLA. No, you see, it's just that I'm a *drunk*.

GRACE. Dear.

CARLA. I'm a drunk and I've been passed out on that sofa all day.

GRACE. Dear.

CARLA. No, it's true. Apparently I have a terrible drinking problem.

GRACE. There's just no need.

CARLA. And I'm also, it seems, a *prostitute*. A drunkard and a prostitute. But thank you for the coffee, Grace.

GRACE. Dear.

CARLA. What sort of casserole did you bring us?

Beat.

PURDY. There seems to be some confusion on this matter of a *casserole*.

Pause.

GRACE. Mr Purdy, did you know that it takes sixteen muscles to frown and only two to smile?

PURDY. Huh.

A kitchen timer rings offstage.

GRACE. Oh dear. The oven. Preheating it. Yes. I'll come back.

GRACE *goes*.

CARLA. Sorry.

PURDY. No.

CARLA. Yes.

PURDY. No. I'll go.

CARLA. No. Sit.

PURDY. No. It was… *remiss* of me –

CARLA. No. It's very kind.

PURDY. Nonetheless.

CARLA. No. I'm serious. Sit.

PURDY. No. I'm sometimes not the best judge of these situations.

CARLA. No, well, who *is*?

PURDY. So I have to rely on your candour.

CARLA. No. I'm trying to say –

PURDY. No, because if you are being – if you're simply *indulging* me –

CARLA. I'm very sorry.

PURDY. – then there's really no point.

CARLA. No. But you have to understand that after a certain amount of time –

PURDY. No. I understand.

CARLA. There's only so much *grief* that a person can – can – can – you know –

PURDY. Yes.

CARLA. I don't know, *ingest*.

PURDY. Yes.

CARLA. So if I come off seeming like some sort of insupportable *cunt* and, well, fantastic now I've managed to work the word cunt into a sentence within three minutes of meeting you.

PURDY. I know the word.

CARLA. And these *casseroles,* these *grief cass–* do you *need* a casserole dish? Seriously, take all you need.

PURDY. No.

CARLA. There's a line around the block. I swear to God this long line all these long faces all these *vultures* with their oven mitts and their Tupperware converging on the house. *Vulture* casserole, they oughta call it.

PURDY. Right.

CARLA. Not to be cold-blooded, but… *show's over.* All right? Go *home.* Remember *life?* Remember *living people?* Lars's commander and his wife were here three weeks ago to present the medal and *Grace*, well, you've had the pleasure of meeting Grace.

PURDY. Yes.

CARLA. And there's a *photographer* to, I don't know, *record* the event for posterity, I guess, and I politely *decline*, ya know, I'd actually rather not have to smile for the camera as I'm being handed this morbid little piece of *jewellery*, but Grace – you met Grace – God bless her, she's *right there.* She's on *top* of it, bless her little heart, and they say so how about we get a shot of his mother and I tell you Grace pops up like she's just won a game of *bingo*, she's standing by the fireplace with the other *vampires*, and they're checking the light with one of those meters and Grace suddenly makes a little noise, a little *squeak* like a little *prairie dog*, and she pulls out a mirror and touches up her *lipstick.* And you know, what a valuable *lesson.* No matter how horrifying the situation, it's always important to *look your best.*

Small pause.

Anyway. You'll understand if I'm not quite as gracious as I should be.

PURDY. You don't remember me, do you?

Long pause.

CARLA (*lying*). No, of course. No, I – of course I –

PURDY. It's all right.

CARLA. No, wait, I – remind me?

PURDY. From the hospital.

CARLA (*still lying*). Ohhhh. Right.

PURDY. It's all right.

CARLA. You – you – you – you're the *chaplain*?

PURDY. No.

CARLA. Wait a minute.

PURDY. Don't worry.

CARLA. No, I remember –

PURDY. I would honestly be surprised if you did.

CARLA. The Military Hospital?

PURDY. It's okay.

CARLA. When are you talking about?

PURDY. July.

CARLA. Well. I mean –

PURDY. We talked one day.

CARLA. I was... *there* in July.

PURDY. Same time as me.

CARLA. Right. And – and – and – and... we talked?

PURDY. I... *didn't*, really. *You* talked. About *snakes*?

CARLA. Wait. I'm talking about the Twenty-third at Fort Irwin.

PURDY. I remember it very clearly.

Pause. CARLA *shakes her head.*

CARLA (*gently*). Um… I don't think so.

PURDY. You had a white bathrobe with blue flowers.

He indicates his lapel, where the flowers would have been on her.

CARLA. *Snakes?*

PURDY. Three snakes. That come out of a jar.

CARLA. I – I – No.

PURDY. I didn't fully understand the significance. I thought you might remember.

CARLA. Mmm-mm. No.

PURDY. Doesn't matter.

CARLA. I wish I did.

PURDY. Presumptuous of me to think.

CARLA. You came to visit *me*. In the hospital.

PURDY. I was there myself.

Small pause.

I lost my hand. (*Showing her.*) Here.

CARLA (*gasps, noticing for the first time*). Oh! (*Begins to laugh.*) Oh my God. I… I'm sorry. *Ouch.* Jesus. I didn't even – *lost it*? *Whoops.* Don't you remember where you *put it*?

PURDY. I know, it's –

CARLA (*embarrassed*). I'm sorry. That's – it's – that was –

PURDY. It's a little creepy.

CARLA. No.

PURDY. Maybe.

CARLA. Maybe a little.

PURDY. It's fibreglass.

CARLA. I didn't even notice.

PURDY. Nice of you to say that.

CARLA. I didn't.

PURDY. Purely cosmetic. Which you might take as a measure of my personal vanity. Still, the best of several unappealing options. And you can bend the fingers. To various positions.

CARLA. And how did it – ?

PURDY. Buried ordnance.

CARLA. I see.

PURDY. Stupid mistake. One among many.

CARLA. It's really only the colour that's noticeable.

PURDY. Not a perfect match, no.

CARLA. No. It's a little –

PURDY. Swarthy, yes. The choices were limited. I've thought of painting it. To even things out.

CARLA. That might work.

PURDY. Unfortunately, *being* right-handed –

CARLA. *Whoops.*

PURDY. Bit of a challenge.

CARLA. Right.

PURDY. But. When my dexterity improves. With the left.

CARLA. That's funny. I could never play the piano *before*.

PURDY. What's that?

CARLA. Nothing.

PURDY. I don't understand.

CARLA. Old joke.

PURDY. Don't know it.

CARLA. Never mind.

PURDY. No, please.

CARLA. It's a terrible... it's – man loses his hands and the doctor sews them back on and after the surgery the man says doctor will I be able to play the piano when I recover and the doctor says I don't see why not and the man says that's funny I could never, ya know... play the piano... before. Stupid joke.

PURDY. Actually, I *did* play the piano. But I can see the humour in that.

Pause.

So you don't remember me.

CARLA. Maybe your face.

PURDY. Right.

CARLA. You have to understand, there are a couple of days for which I can't fully –

PURDY. Account.

CARLA. With the medication. And everything. So it would be a little surprising.

PURDY. If you did. Remember.

CARLA. Sorry.

PURDY. You asked me to untie your hands.

Beat.

CARLA. Oh.

PURDY. We were talking. *You* were talking, I suppose is the way to say it. And you said once the snakes are out of the jar how do you get them back in? And then you said can you untie my hands.

CARLA. They were, yes.

PURDY. They're trying to kill me, you said. And I said I didn't
think that was right. I said that no one was going to hurt you
that you were perfectly safe as far as I could tell so I said I
can't do that for you, that I wished I could but that they
didn't want you to hurt yourself so I thought it wasn't my
place to do that. You looked at me. I couldn't tell if you
really saw me. I said I thought I should call the doctor and
you said go fuck yourself. Then you said I'll hate you for as
long as you live. Then I left the room.

There is a long silence.

CARLA. See, no one ever bothers to tell you that a military
transport isn't going to have a *beverage service*. Whoever
heard of a seven-hour flight without any sort of *reasonably
stocked beverage service*? Fucking military. No wonder Lars
had a stick up his – Sorry. He's your friend. But, yes when
you've been on a plane for seven hours without the beverage
service and they set you down in the middle of some *desert*,
in *July* and they say to you we'll need to get things under way
as soon as we can so go ahead relax, get four hours of sleep,
we just need to get things started at the chapel at oh-nine-
hundred but if there's anything you need you let us know and
you say well you know since you bring it up there might be
one little thing actually I'm just a little parched you know just
something maybe to take the edge off is that the sort of thing
that one might be able to find at three in the morning in the
middle of this godforsaken – and then of course the
embarrassed looks as you realise that *whoops* you happen to
be talking to the fucking *chaplain*. I mean, would it be too
much to sport the traditional collar so that a person doesn't
make a complete *jackass* of – ? So nine a.m. After spending
the night in front of the ice-cold window unit thinking gee
remember how every time Lars would come home from a
tour how he'd spend the first week showing you everything
that you'd done wrong around the house, tugging on the
pleats of those curtains and down on his hands and knees with
a comb, a black-rubber pocket comb *combing the fringe* on

that rug gotta get the *fringe* straight gotta maintain that *fringe*
at ninety degrees look sharp there, carpet. You know, Carla,
you know, baby, all it takes is a little attention to detail,
walking around in his jockey shorts whistling the 'Halls of
Montezuma'. So. Nine a.m. And they take you to this little
room and now you're really starting to feel like you could use
that beverage, you know, you've just about hit the point
where a little nail polish, a little hairspray might just do the
trick, a little Windex maybe but they take you to the room and
you want to say *Larsen*, you pathetic – *Larsen* don't you
know a Lutheran name when you see one? For Christ's sake
how fucking stupid do you have to – ? *No open casket in the
Lutheran church*, okay? Consult one of your many manuals.
This *is* my *husband* here, all right? This *is* the piece of shit
himself here in this aluminum box this display case who used
to hit me across the face with a rolled-up newspaper like you
hit a dog this embalmed asshole who used to do this to me in
front of our *child* could we grant him please his privacy and
close the fucking *lid*? And then they hand you this plastic bag
this see-through vinyl pouch for your entertainment little
packet of nostalgia down memory lane with his Timex watch
and the pocketknife and the cheap J.C. Penney *wallet* and
you're thinking well as long as there's a lull a little break in
the action maybe *I'm* in here somewhere maybe tucked away
here in the back behind the credit cards me and Thor maybe
hey Lars how's the wife and kids well lemme show ya but
now wait a minute, hang on a sec, funny, I don't recall *this*
event this particular *Kodak moment* with the little slanty-eyed
girl on my husband's lap what is she fourteen, fifteen with all
the mascara it's hard to tell wearing nothing but sequins and
glue and a smile right there on his lap in the little high heels
legs crossed and he's giving the photographer the big thumbs-
up with one hand while the other squeezes the little yellow
titty that he is *licking*. Or maybe she spilled her drink and he's
helping clean her off because he's such a thoughtful man,
your husband, the same man who has refused to fuck *you* for
the last two years because you're too *disgusting* to fuck he
says, you smell like a distillery. Who in their right mind
would want to fuck you? What happened you used to make

an effort you used to have a little pride and I say well you certainly know how to charm the ladies, big boy, you certainly know how to make a woman feel special so when you see this poor little fifteen-year-old whore in a miniskirt sitting on the lap of your dead husband the prick laid out in a tin can at the other end of the room, *well*. When you're looking at that and you've been wanting a drink for the past twenty-four hours, thirty-six when you factor in the day spent packing, with your son trying to figure out how to mourn the man who used to give him a bloody nose if he tracked mud in the house I mean when you add all that up I guess it's not unreasonable to assume that something had to give.

Pause. THOR *comes down the hallway wearing a werewolf mask and hands. He passes calmly through and exits to the kitchen.*

PURDY. I'm sorry he passed away.

CARLA. Thank you.

PURDY. And for your son. That's *Thor*?

CARLA. Yes.

PURDY. For him, too.

From the kitchen, we hear a crash and GRACE *screams.* THOR *comes through the room again, calmly as before, and exits up the hall.*

May I make an observation? You seem to be the sort of person who has a lot of negative feelings about herself. You tend to feel like maybe you've done a lot of things wrong. Am I right about that?

CARLA (*shrugs*). Possibly.

PURDY. I say this because until recently I had very negative thoughts about *myself*. I had begun to think that all of the things that I wanted, all of the things that I enjoyed must be bad and that I must be a bad person for wanting them. It's hard to say *exactly why* I felt this way. I don't know. I never had a lot of friends, and my father would tell me, with some frequency, that I *was* a bad person. That I was selfish and greedy and thought only of myself, not of the other person, that I didn't take the feelings of others into consideration, and that made *me* a bad person. And naturally I believed him because he was my father and why would your father tell you something that wasn't true? So I said to him how am I supposed to become a better person? How do I achieve that? And he said simply listen to your conscience. And I was confused. I said is my *conscience* the same as my *soul*? No, he said, your conscience is different. Your *conscience* is a little angel that sits right here on your shoulder and he tells you when you've done something bad. It's sitting there right now. It never goes to sleep and it never gets tired. I see. So I said what if you want to do something even though your conscience tells you not to? And he said that's what we call wickedness. But I said, what if the conscience makes a mistake? What if it takes over and it makes you feel bad about everything you love? Everything perfect or beautiful? And he said it never makes a mistake. *Never*, I said? He said think about this: he said why do you think people who set a building on fire always come back to the scene of the crime? Why else would they do that? They don't *want* to go to *jail*, do they? No, their conscience *makes* them come back. He said their conscience knows it was wrong, and it has a little tiny whip and it whips them and whips them until they go back to that burning building to see how wicked they were. And I thought about this for a few seconds. I really had to think. Because that didn't seem right to me. So I thought about it very hard and after a few seconds I turned to him and I said –

CARLA. They go back because the burning building is beautiful.

Beat.

PURDY (*smiles*). That's exactly what I said. I didn't get my allowance that week.

They both smile and stare at the floor. PURDY *laughs.*

CARLA. What?

PURDY. That's funny. I could never play the piano *before*.

Pause. They smile and begin laughing. It goes on for a bit.

What an astonishing volume of horseshit people expect you
to swallow. Do you know what I mean? What a staggering,
towering load of pure unreconstituted crap, delivered to your
door every day by everyone you know, all these respectable
citizens trundling up to your front door with their enormous
creaking carts full of shit, each one with a blindfold and a
clothespin on their nose, each one deluded, each one
convinced that they are in fact hauling an equal quantity of
diamonds. And each one offering you a little spoonful of
their precious horseshit. Here. Have a taste. Today's your
lucky day. With each spoonful you get a free cartload. Free
mountain of shit. Shit *volcano*. C'mon. Dig in. Doesn't *taste*
like shit. I swear. Tastes great. Tastes like diamonds and
rubies and pimento cheese and comfy sofas and football
games and beer and rock and roll and *Playboy* magazine and
the *Tonight Show* and the Hollywood Squares and Hallmark
cards and little sayings in needlepoint on their pillows and
art museums and the theatre and church on Sunday. You can
mould the horseshit into any shape you want. But when you
pop it in your mouth and swallow it down it still comes out
horseshit. And not a one of them, not a *one* has the courage
to unbuckle their harness and leave their cartload of
horseshit behind for two seconds and experience a single
uninterrupted moment of genuine beauty.

Beat.

CARLA. I'm not really sure I have any idea what it is you're
talking about. But I'm almost certain that I agree with it.

PURDY. I'm trying to say that it might be a good idea for you
not to blame yourself so much. That's what I decided. A few
years ago I decided to take that little conscience, the one that
my father said had been sitting on my shoulder all those
years, sitting there with his little whip, I decided to take that

conscience off my shoulder and snap its neck just like a little sparrow's neck. And I think you might feel better if you did the same thing.

Pause.

CARLA. Maybe you should stay for dinner.

PURDY. That would be nice.

THOR *enters on his way to the kitchen.*

CARLA (*to* THOR). Hey.

THOR. Hey what?

CARLA. That clock is crooked.

THOR *climbs the ladder and begins straightening the clock.*

You're sort of different from most of Lars's friends.

PURDY. Is that good or bad?

CARLA. I don't know.

PURDY. How would you characterise his friends?

CARLA. I... well, I don't – It's sort of difficult to – in *general*, and I'm not including you in this, but in *general* I guess I'd have to characterise them as – as – *generally* a bunch of *motherfucking assholes*.

They laugh and smile. And in the next second the ladder is toppling over with THOR *on it.*

PURDY. Whoa whoa whoa   CARLA. Hey hey no no no –
whoa *watch it – Look out!!*   Thor Thor – *Watch what*
Look out!!   *you're – !!*

PURDY *springs from the sofa and without thinking reaches out to* THOR *with his false hand.* THOR *grabs for it as he falls and pulls it, strap and all, off of* PURDY's *arm.* CARLA *screams again.* THOR *hits the ground and realises what he is holding. He lets out a yelp and throws the hand on the sofa.* GRACE *rushes in. Now* CARLA *sees the hand and begins to laugh uncontrollably at* THOR's *distress.*

THOR (*to CARLA*). *It's not funny! No it's not, you fat cow! Shut up, you pig!!! I don't know why you're laughing because it's NOT FUNNY!!*

GRACE. What is it? What – I told you, Thor, I told you *several times* that this is what could happen but you chose not to listen to me and now just look. Thor! Not so loud!

PURDY (*to GRACE*). I'm sorry, ma'am. The boy was on the ladder and I thought I was helping but apparently I just complicated the situation.

PURDY *retrieves his hand from the sofa.* CARLA *cannot stop laughing. She holds her stomach, then puts her hand to her mouth. She looks around and quickly grabs a wastebasket, then throws up into it, which is to say, she turns* downstage *and we watch the vomit come out of her mouth. The others see this. Long pause.*

GRACE. Thor, could you take that ladder out, please?

THOR. Why?

GRACE. Thor.

THOR. Why do I have to do it?

GRACE. I warned you something like this might happen.

PURDY. I can do it.

GRACE (*to* PURDY). I think it's probably time we say goodnight.

PURDY. Uhh. All right.

GRACE. It was so kind of you to go out of your way like this.

PURDY. You're very welcome.

GRACE. We're just about to sit down to dinner.

PURDY. Right.

GRACE. But it was so nice to meet you.

PURDY. Yes.

GRACE. And if you're ever this way again.

PURDY. I will.

GRACE. I hope so.

PURDY. I definitely will.

GRACE. Good.

PURDY. Definitely.

GRACE. Good. So.

   He doesn't move.

CARLA. Can somebody get me a glass of water?

PURDY. Uhhhh –

GRACE. Thor?

THOR (*to* GRACE). I'm not your *slave*.

   Pause. THOR *goes to the kitchen.*

GRACE (*to* PURDY). Goodnight.

PURDY. I hope I didn't –

GRACE. You've been very kind.

PURDY. No, because I truly… I feel – perhaps, some
   responsibility –

GRACE. No.

PURDY. It being the dinner hour and all.

GRACE. Everything's fine.

   CARLA *feels another small wave of nausea. She picks up
   the wastebasket and exits up the hall.*

PURDY (*to* GRACE). Um. Goodnight.

GRACE. Goodnight.

He exits. After a few seconds, THOR *returns with a glass of water. He sees that* CARLA *has gone. He sets the water down and picks up the ladder, but rather than take it away he sets it up again. He begins to climb it.*

No. Thor, no. Don't do that. No. Thor? I'm serious, now. I mean it. Don't go up there. *Thor?*

He reaches the clock and makes the tiniest adjustment in its angle.

All right then. Thank you.

THOR *descends, folds the ladder, and carries it out of the room. After a moment,* CARLA *enters.*

CARLA. Do you have the Milk of Magnesia?

GRACE. Maybe you should lie down.

CARLA. Maybe I will.

GRACE. Maybe you should.

CARLA. Do we have any crackers?

GRACE. Well, I may have eaten the last of them. There's bread.

CARLA *shakes her head. Pause.*

How is Dr Wilborn's leg doing?

CARLA. How is *what*?

GRACE. Dr Wilborn.

CARLA. His *leg*?

GRACE. I wondered if he was still using the cane.

CARLA. ...I don't know.

GRACE. You remember that he had phlebitis.

CARLA. I forgot.

GRACE. That's why he had the cane.

CARLA. Well, I didn't notice a cane.

GRACE. Perhaps it's improved.

CARLA. Not today anyway.

GRACE. But it's strange because I saw him at Kroger's yesterday and he *had* the cane.

Pause.

You didn't see Dr Wilborn, did you?

CARLA (*appalled*). *Yes.*

GRACE. I'm trying to be helpful.

CARLA. What an interesting *method* you've chosen.

GRACE. I'll pick up some crackers at the market tomorrow.

CARLA. I'm going to go.

GRACE. The Pastor can take me. Rather than your visit.

CARLA. I'm fine.

GRACE. Well. Obviously not. All right. Crackers, milk and butter. And laundry detergent.

Pause.

What about tampons? Shall I pick some up for you?

CARLA *stares at her.*

Do you need some? Or do you have enough?

CARLA. I have enough.

GRACE. I know you do.

CARLA. Then why did you ask?

GRACE. Well, I've noticed that on average you buy a new box every two months or so. And for the last three months I've noticed that the number of tampons in the box in your bathroom cupboard has remained constant.

CARLA. Has it?

GRACE. That's what I've noticed.

CARLA (*bitter laugh*). Grace, I gotta tell you. This *melodrama* that you have cooked up, this *soap opera* – this *mystery novel* that you have concocted with me as the central character, well, look, we all need a hobby, all right? And I'm sure it's a creative outlet for your smutty little imagination but I've gotta tell ya one of the key things is you want to keep the plot line *plausible*. Gotta keep your facts straight or your audience isn't gonna let you get away with – ya know, if it's over three months since your hero died and the hero's wife hadn't seen him for six months prior to that, see, they'd say you know, the *timeline* just doesn't quite work out, *unless*, wait a minute, see, I didn't realise – that's the genius of your version, Grace, you throw in a *miracle*, now that's a *twist*. That's a *new one*. Like the New Testament. How about if from *beyond the grave* the holy spirit of the dead husband pays a secret visit to the central character and no one believes her, I think ya really got something there, Grace, keep up the good work, and *no*, I don't know what's wrong with me, and *yes* if you believe what I think you're implying, then *yes*, you are losing your mind, and *no*, I don't need any *tampons*.

GRACE. Would you like me to call the young man for you? You'll have to tell me which one it was. I was never introduced. But he does have the right to know.

CARLA (*still calm*). Your son liked to *fuck* prostitutes, Grace, not *marry* them.

GRACE. Lars would be so sad to hear you use that language.

CARLA. Good thing he died, then, rather than hear me say the word *fuck*.

GRACE. Dear, you make me want to cry.

CARLA. Don't cry, Grace. Maybe he'll be *resurrected*.

GRACE. You like to be hurtful and that's because of the alcohol.

CARLA. Of course it is.

GRACE. And then to allow Thor to lie for you. I don't consider that loving your child.

CARLA picks up the glass of water and hurls it at the wall, shattering it. She picks up the fork. She pushes it against her neck.

CARLA. *HOW ABOUT IF I STAB MYSELF, GRACE??!! HOW ABOUT IF I DO THAT??!! HUH??!! IF I STAB MYSELF WOULD THAT POSSIBLY FOR FUCK'S SAKE POSSIBLY GET YOU FOR FIFTEEN MINUTES OFF MY GODDAMN BACK?? FIFTEEN MINUTES OF QUIET IS THAT SO MUCH TO FUCKING ASK????*

She flings the fork across the room. Silence.

GRACE. No one wants you to hurt yourself, dear. You know we don't want that.

THOR *enters.*

THOR. Are we still going to eat?

GRACE. Dinner's going to be a little late tonight.

THOR. I'm hungry.

GRACE. Why don't you have a nice bowl of cereal? Wouldn't you like that? You could take it to your room.

THOR. We don't have any milk.

Pause. THOR *doesn't move.*

GRACE. Your mother and I are having a conversation, Thor.

THOR. What about?

GRACE. That's not important.

THOR. Tell me.

GRACE. Thor.

THOR. Tell me.

GRACE. We don't give *orders.*

THOR. Tell me.

GRACE. Thor.

THOR. Tell me.

GRACE. No.

THOR. Tell me.

GRACE. I want you to stop.

THOR. Tell me.

GRACE. Thor.

THOR. Tell me.

GRACE. No.

THOR. Tell me.

GRACE. You're behaving like a spoiled chil–

THOR (*suddenly bellowing*). *TELL MEEEEEE!!!*

 Pause.

GRACE. All right then. Your mother is going to have a child.

THOR. You're a liar.

GRACE. No.

THOR. Yes you are.

GRACE. You asked for the truth and I told you.

THOR. I hate you.

 Beat.

GRACE. I think you know we don't use the word hate in this
 house.

THOR. Oh so it's your house now.

GRACE. No.

THOR. How much did you pay for it?

GRACE. Hate is a very strong word.

THOR. What if I said I wish you were dead?

GRACE. Well.

Pause.

All right then.

The lights fade to black.

End of Act One.

ACT TWO

*Five-thirty a.m., standard time. The house is completely dark
once again. A dog barks outside. After a few seconds,* CARLA*'s
silhouette appears in the hallway. She wears only her
nightgown. She braces herself against the wall, apparently in
pain. She slowly makes her way across the room and exits to the
kitchen. A few more seconds go by, then she reappears carrying
a purse. She turns on a lamp, which illuminates only a tabletop
and her face.*

*She empties the entire contents of the purse onto the table. She
opens two different drawers and closes them in quick
succession. She goes to a closet and finds her coat, then feels
around in the pockets. She opens a cabinet and pulls out a
phone book. She tosses it aside and heads back toward the
closet.*

At that moment, GRACE *turns on another lamp. She has been
sitting in a chair across the room, wearing her bathrobe and
yellow rubber gloves.*

CARLA *gasps, freezes.*

GRACE. I don't think you'll find it there.

CARLA. Find what?

GRACE. The Yellow Pages.

CARLA. Where?

GRACE. In the closet.

CARLA. Why would the Yellow Pages be in the closet?

GRACE. I don't think it would be.

CARLA. I'm not looking for the Yellow Pages.

GRACE. I was mistaken.

Pause. They stare at each other.

I startled you.

CARLA. No.

GRACE. I'm sorry.

CARLA. You didn't.

GRACE. I should have spoken sooner.

CARLA. I wasn't startled.

GRACE. To let you know.

CARLA. Know what?

GRACE. That I was sitting here.

CARLA. I don't care.

GRACE. As a courtesy.

CARLA. Sit wherever you want.

GRACE. I'm sorry.

CARLA. I wasn't startled.

GRACE. Because I noticed you looking in the cabinet.

CARLA. So?

GRACE. And the White Pages didn't seem to suit your needs.

CARLA. Why are you *awake*?

GRACE. Well, I suppose it was the coffee. Did you have coffee, too?

CARLA. No.

GRACE. That's a lesson. Never after six. Let that be a *lesson* for me.

CARLA. Go back to sleep.

GRACE. Not *black* coffee. The absence of milk may have been a factor. Undiluted like that. But, as we don't seem to own a *cow*, there we are.

CARLA. A *cow*?

GRACE. For the milk.

CARLA. What are you talking about?

GRACE. Cows make milk.

CARLA. Of course we don't own a *cow*.

GRACE. It was a joke, dear.

CARLA. I don't know why you'd *say* that.

GRACE. Because we're out of milk.

CARLA. I know that.

GRACE. It was said in *jest*.

CARLA. I know, but – but – but – but… I *know*.

GRACE. I know you do.

Pause.

You look pale.

CARLA. I'm tired.

GRACE. Couldn't you sleep?

CARLA. Why are you wearing those gloves?

GRACE. I did some cleaning.

CARLA. In the middle of the night?

GRACE. Since I was awake.

CARLA. All right.

GRACE. As long as I was awake I thought I'd do a little cleaning. (*Thinks*.) Not the *middle* of the night, exactly.

CARLA. No.

GRACE. Rather than sit alone in the dark and do nothing.

CARLA. But you *were* sitting alone in the dark.

GRACE. I took a little break.

Pause.

I'm sorry I startled you.

CARLA. You *didn't*.

GRACE. I would be angry, too.

CARLA. I'm *not* angry.

GRACE. Consternated.

CARLA. *Frustrated.*

GRACE. Because you can't find the Yellow Pages?

CARLA. Because of this *conversation*.

GRACE. Because you're tired.

CARLA. I'm not tired.

GRACE. You said you –

CARLA. No, what I *said* was – all right. Yes. I guess I am.

GRACE. I was looking for the Yellow Pages just the other day.

CARLA. Grace.

GRACE. It *is* frustrating. It seems to have gone missing.

CARLA. Grace. I am not looking for the Yellow Pages.

GRACE. All right.

CARLA. I am not.

GRACE. All right.

CARLA. Looking.

GRACE. All right.

CARLA. For the Yellow Pages.

GRACE. All right.

> CARLA *exits to the hallway. After a few seconds she returns and stares suspiciously at* GRACE.

CARLA. I'm looking for my keys.

GRACE. Your house keys?

CARLA. My keyring with my keys on it.

GRACE. Your *car* keys, then.

CARLA. My *keys*, yes. My keys.

GRACE. Where did you want to go?

CARLA. Have you seen them?

GRACE. I don't think anywhere will be open at this hour of the morning. (*Beat.*) Where were you planning to go?

CARLA. The Stop-N-Go.

GRACE. On K Street?

CARLA. They're not in my coat pocket.

GRACE. The Stop-N-Go won't be open at this hour.

CARLA. They're open twenty-four hours.

GRACE. Not any more. Not since the summer.

CARLA. Or the doughnut shop.

GRACE. To buy doughnuts?

CARLA. To buy milk. We need milk. They sell milk.

> *Pause.*

GRACE. I have your car keys.

CARLA. Where were they?

GRACE. They were in your purse.

CARLA. You took them out of my purse.

GRACE. I was cleaning out the car.

CARLA. My car.

GRACE. Rather than sit idly in the dark.

CARLA. Did you find what you were looking for?

GRACE. I don't understand.

CARLA. In the course of your inspection.

GRACE. Dear.

CARLA. And where are my keys now?

GRACE. They're in my pocket.

Pause.

CARLA. I suppose you can anticipate my next question.

GRACE. Where did you need to go, dear?

THOR *enters, in pyjamas. He turns on the overhead lights.*

THOR. Does the Post Office have to pay you if they lose your mail?

GRACE. Thor.

THOR. They should have to pay you.

GRACE. It's too early.

THOR. So they just steal from you and you can't do anything about it?

GRACE. Please go back to sleep.

CARLA *begins to search through several drawers. They watch her.*

THOR. What's going on?

GRACE. You're going to be very tired if you don't go back to sleep.

THOR. So are you.

GRACE. Please. As a favour to me.

THOR. You first.

> CARLA *exits up the hallway, slamming a door as she goes.*

What's she looking for?

GRACE. The Yellow Pages.

THOR. We don't have one.

GRACE. Of course we do.

THOR. Not any more.

GRACE. What happened to it?

THOR. I used it for something.

GRACE. For what?

THOR. I burned it.

GRACE. Where?

THOR. In the fireplace.

GRACE. Why?

THOR. It was cold.

GRACE. Why didn't you turn up the thermostat?

THOR. Fires are nicer.

GRACE. But we have logs for that purpose.

THOR. Yellow Pages are free.

GRACE. But we need the Yellow Pages.

THOR. But I saved you money.

GRACE. I think you're making this up.

THOR. I don't care.

GRACE. You know the difference between right and wrong. You're not a child.

THOR. Yes I am.

> *Beat.*

GRACE. You know, when people try to be hurtful to others they usually wind up hurting themselves.

THOR. They must not plan very carefully.

There is a crash offstage.

CARLA (*offstage*)....*how can there be no motherfucking YELLOW PAGES ANYWHERE IN THIS MOTHERFUCKING HOUSE!?!?!?*

GRACE. Back to bed, now.

THOR. I'm not sleepy.

GRACE. I'm not discussing it.

THOR. Why is everybody awake?

   CARLA *re-enters, quite agitated.*

CARLA (*to* THOR). Have you seen the extra keys?

THOR. What extra keys?

CARLA. On the metal ring.

THOR. No.

CARLA. They were in that drawer.

THOR. Why are you asking me?

CARLA. Did you move them?

THOR. I didn't know they existed.

CARLA. *They're on a metal ring.*

THOR. So blame *me*.

   CARLA *exits again.*

   Where's she going?

GRACE. No one is going anywhere.

THOR. Nowhere's open to go.

   CARLA *returns.*

CARLA. Give me the keys, Grace.

GRACE. I would think that, at this point the two of us could be more honest with each other.

CARLA. I want my keys.

GRACE. You tell me that you are going to the doughnut shop –

CARLA. No, you're right. You caught me. It's true. I'm going to get gasoline. A gallon of gas and a book of matches and when the two of you go to sleep I'm going to pour the gasoline around your beds and set you both on fire.

GRACE. Thor?

THOR. What?

GRACE. Come here a moment.

THOR. You just told me to go away.

GRACE. Sit down here, please.

THOR. Fine with me.

THOR *sits near* GRACE.

GRACE. I want to tell you something. And I want you to know that I'm telling you this because I think that you are mature enough to understand. I'm not going to give the car keys to your mother because I believe that she has a drinking problem. Do you understand what that means?

THOR. No hablo inglés.

CARLA *laughs and exits to the kitchen. Banging noises are heard.*

GRACE. Yes. And I'm fairly certain that she wants the car keys so that she can go and find herself some more liquor. But I think that if I was to give her the car keys that I would be helping her to hurt herself, and I don't think that would make me a very nice person. You understand that, don't you?

THOR. No comprendo.

GRACE. Well, I know you're being this way because you love your mother and you don't want to hurt her and I think that's nice of you. But I love your mother, too. We just have different ways of showing it. And I hope someday you'll understand that and then we could be friends. Because I'd like for us to be friends.

THOR. Why, are your friends all dead?

CARLA *re-enters*.

CARLA. Give me the goddamn keys. I'll take the car, I'll go get my *liquor* and I'll drink myself to sleep.

GRACE. I could let you do that. I could. But it wouldn't just be *one* person that was drinking the liquor, now would it?

THOR. No, I'd have some, too.

GRACE. And I think we ought to consider *that* person as well.

CARLA. *How*, Grace? You explain it to me.

GRACE. How what?

CARLA. If that's what you believe. Let's hear your analysis.

GRACE. This is not the time.

CARLA. Lay it out for me.

GRACE. At the proper time.

CARLA. Because I'm frankly *stumped*. Because you see, I was under the impression that a person would have to take certain *steps*. Do you follow?

GRACE. Thor?

CARLA. And if I *haven't* taken those steps, Grace – And I *haven't* taken them –

GRACE (*to* THOR). Back to bed, please.

CARLA. *I haven't taken them*. Do you hear what I am saying? *I haven't*. So you explain it to me. Explain the medical mystery.

GRACE. It's not really such a mystery, is it?

CARLA. You're either calling me a *liar* or you're calling me a *whore*. I'd just like to know which one it is. A or B.

THOR. Or both.

GRACE. Thor.

CARLA. Right. A *lying whore*. A, B or C. And while you're thinking that one over you can give me my keys.

GRACE. Not in your condition.

CARLA. And by the way let's not forget that you've got half a bottle of *my* vodka in your room. I don't *need* to go out for *liquor*.

GRACE. I poured that down the toilet.

CARLA *laughs*.

I do these things because I love you and I care about you.

CARLA. Wow. Thank God you don't *hate* me.

GRACE. I don't hate people. I hate certain *actions*. But never a person. I try to love all people.

THOR. What about Hitler?

CARLA. I am going to ask you one last time.

THOR (*to* GRACE). You love Hitler.

CARLA. *Shut the fuck up, you little asshole*.

THOR. Go ahead, hit me. See if I care.

CARLA *grabs her stomach in pain*. GRACE *notices*.

GRACE. No one said anything about *hitting*.

THOR (*to* CARLA). I'm not afraid of *you*.

GRACE. We do not *hit* in this house.

THOR. So let's go outside.

GRACE. There are other ways of settling differences.

CARLA (*to* GRACE, *in pain*). *Love*. Yeah, you're *full* of love. You're the *goddess* of love. Thank God you never felt any *love* you'd burst into *flames*, you dried-up sack of twigs.

GRACE (*hurt*). Well, I suppose we've finally hit bottom.

THOR. Don't hit *my* bottom.

CARLA. And now that we're at the bottom you can give me the keys.

GRACE. I think, when you look back, in the *future* –

CARLA. But we're not in the *future*. We're in the present, okay? This is the *present. NOW GIVE ME THE FUCKING KEYS.*

The doorbell rings. All freeze. Then, very softly, a knock on the door. No one moves. Seconds pass. The knock is heard again. THOR *moves.*

GRACE. No. We do not answer the door at this hour.

THOR *sits.* CARLA *starts to exit. We hear the door opening. All freeze.*

PURDY (*from off*). Hello?

No one knows what to do.

Hello?

PURDY *enters the room. He carries a paper bag and a small cardboard box.* CARLA *attempts to cover herself. Throughout the following they all remain as calm as possible.*

Good morning. I saw the lights on.

They exchange looks.

I was wondering if I might interest anyone in a doughnut? I have a dozen here. Dozen doughnuts.

GRACE. I don't think so. Thank you.

PURDY. I'm sorry. I knocked. Perhaps not loudly enough.

GRACE. I suppose we didn't hear.

PURDY. I saw the lights on. So I knocked.

GRACE. Yes.

PURDY. Did you know your door was unlocked?

GRACE. No.

PURDY. Probably be a good idea to lock it. As a precaution. I
also rang the doorbell. Does the doorbell not work?

GRACE. It works.

PURDY. Oh. All right.

Pause.

Actually, I'm not telling the truth. It's not quite the full
dozen, since I helped myself to two of them already.
However, the balance remains. Of the doughnuts, that is. The
standard glazed variety.

GRACE. I'm sorry, I'm afraid you'll have to come back at a
later hour.

PURDY. Oh, I'm sorry. I misunderstood.

GRACE. No need to apologise.

PURDY. The lights were on.

GRACE. And thank you for stopping.

PURDY. And I heard voices so I assumed – did I *wake* you?

GRACE. No.

PURDY. I apologise if I did.

GRACE. You didn't.

PURDY. I didn't think so. With the lights on and the voices.

GRACE. But thank you for looking in.

PURDY. I was afraid there might be some sort of problem.

Pause.

Is there some sort of problem?

GRACE. I'm really going to have to ask you to visit us some *other* time.

PURDY. I'm terribly sorry.

GRACE. Another time.

PURDY. Yes. Sorry.

Pause.

So what time shall we say?

GRACE. It *is* five-thirty in the morning.

PURDY. I apologise.

GRACE. No. *Don't apologise.*

PURDY. All right.

GRACE. You do understand –

PURDY. I do, yes, however, I feel some implication that I have done something *wrong*, something *inappropriate*, yet as I am attempting to apologise for whatever that wrong may *be*, you insist that I should *not* apologise, and in so doing you put me in a rather awkward situation.

GRACE. I see. Yes. Your apology is accepted.

PURDY. All right. So another time, then?

GRACE. Goodnight.

PURDY. Or morning, really. Yes. Good.

Pause. He starts to go.

THOR. Can I have a doughnut?

GRACE. No.

PURDY. No, I don't think –

GRACE. No doughnuts now.

PURDY. No. (*To* GRACE.) It's early for doughnuts.

GRACE (*to* PURDY). *No. Let's not –*

PURDY. No. You're right.

GRACE. No. Goodnight.

PURDY. Better not.

GRACE. No.

PURDY. No.

GRACE. No.

PURDY. No.

GRACE. No.

PURDY. So.

CARLA (*to* PURDY). Wait. (*Beat.*) I need you to drive me
    somewhere.

    Pause.

GRACE. Dear.

CARLA. Will you drive me somewhere?

PURDY. Me?

CARLA. Yes.

GRACE. Dear.

PURDY. Now?

CARLA. Yes.

PURDY. Well –

GRACE. No.

CARLA. Please.

GRACE. Mr Purdy, we have been having a discussion. A
    Family Discussion.

CARLA. As soon as possible.

GRACE. Into which you have been innocently drafted –
(*Continues*.)

PURDY (*overlapping*). Well –

CARLA. This *is* my house, Grace. It's *my* house. – (*Continues*.)

GRACE. – and with which we needn't burden you.

CARLA. – And I will speak to whoever I want.

PURDY. The thing is –

CARLA. When I am *in* my house.

GRACE. So if I may ask you once again –

PURDY (*to* CARLA). The thing is, I don't have a *car*.

   Pause.

CARLA. *What?*

PURDY. I don't have one.

CARLA. You don't have a *car*?

PURDY. Don't *you* have a car?

CARLA. We *have* a car.

PURDY (*to* CARLA). Then perhaps *you* could drive.

GRACE (*quickly*). No no no.

CARLA (*to* GRACE). *He* can drive.

PURDY. Drive *your* car?

CARLA (*to* PURDY). You can drive.

PURDY (*re:* GRACE). Or *she* could.

GRACE. I don't *drive*.

CARLA (*re:* PURDY). But *he* can.

PURDY. I *know* how to drive.

GRACE. Dear.

PURDY. Do you know the car's *transmission*?

CARLA (*perplexed*)....*specifically?*

PURDY. I'm saying that it might not be possible. If standard transmission. Given the current situation with my *hand*.

CARLA. Oh.

PURDY. The gear shift located, as it is, to the *right* of the steering column.

CARLA. Oh.

PURDY. I'm sorry.

CARLA. Oh.

PURDY. Standard, then, is it?

THOR. Four on the floor.

PURDY. That seems inadvisable.

Pause. All stare at the floor.

(*To* CARLA.) Where did you need to go?

CARLA. Nowhere.

GRACE (*gently*). You see, we were under the *impression* that she wanted to go to the *doughnut shop*.

PURDY. Well, I did *bring* doughnuts.

CARLA. For *milk*. I wanted milk.

PURDY. Oh, and I… happen to have milk, as well.

He removes a small carton of milk from the paper bag. CARLA *is rigid, miserable.*

GRACE. Well. That's a problem solved then, isn't it?

PURDY. Feel free to –

GRACE. You have your milk now, dear.

PURDY (*to* CARLA). Have I complicated the situation?

GRACE (*genuinely, not sarcastic*). Would you like me to get you a glass?

CARLA. I can get it. (*To* PURDY.) Thank you.

CARLA *takes the milk and starts toward the kitchen. After a few steps, her knees buckle and she falls face down on the floor.* PURDY *and* GRACE *move awkwardly to help her. The following lines rapidly overlap:*

| GRACE. All right. Let's see. I think it's probably best if we get you back into bed. (*To* PURDY.) Would you give us a hand, here please? If you could? | PURDY. Oh gosh. Careful there. I – sorry. Let me see if I can – maybe I should – (*To* GRACE.) Yes, ma'am. | CARLA. I'm fine. I'm perfectly fine. I don't *need* a glass, Grace. I can drink it out of the *carton*, for Christ's sake. |

PURDY *lifts* CARLA *from the floor, holding her in his arms.*

PURDY. Here we go.

CARLA (*not entirely coherent*). People drink out of the *carton*, Grace, that's what they *do*.

GRACE. Have you got her?

PURDY. Yes, ma'am.

CARLA (*in the clear*). Why does that make me a *bad person*?

GRACE. Let's go back to bed, dear.

PURDY. You're not a bad person.

CARLA (*to* PURDY). I need you to take me somewhere.

GRACE. He will.

PURDY (*to* CARLA). I don't have a car.

GRACE. Back to bed.

CARLA. No. Bathroom.

GRACE. All right. The bathroom, then.

CARLA *is in* PURDY*'s arms. He carries her up the hallway as* GRACE *leads the way.* THOR *is left alone. He goes to the box of doughnuts and takes one, then retires to the corner to eat.* PURDY *returns. He sits next to the telephone. He removes a small card from his breast pocket, picks up the telephone and dials. After listening, he speaks:*

PURDY. Nine three two three Greenwillow. Yes. As soon as possible.

He hangs up and puts the card away. Several seconds pass. GRACE *returns.*

GRACE. Thank you.

PURDY. You're welcome.

GRACE. I think we'll be fine now.

PURDY *does not move.*

I imagine it must be chilly outside.

PURDY. A bit, yes, ma'am.

GRACE. You should have a sweater.

PURDY. It's sweater weather.

Beat.

GRACE. It's *wetter*?

PURDY. *Sweater.*

GRACE. *I* said sweater.

PURDY. You said *sweater.* I said *sweater weather.*

GRACE. Oh, *sweater* weather.

PURDY. Yes.

GRACE. Not it's *wetter* weather.

PURDY. *Sweater* weather.

GRACE. I would have offered an umbrella.

PURDY. No.

GRACE. *Sweater* weather.

PURDY. Yes.

GRACE. Sort of a tongue-twister. Sweater weather sweater
  weather.

PURDY. Yes.

GRACE. So, I think we'll be fine, now.

PURDY. Good.

  He still does not move.

GRACE. You don't own a car?

PURDY. No, ma'am.

GRACE. In this day and age?

PURDY. Never owned one.

GRACE. You are an *iconoclast*.

PURDY. I came by train.

GRACE (*confused*). But, last night – ?

PURDY. I *arrived* last night.

GRACE. No, but *after* the train?

PURDY. I walked.

GRACE. From the *train station*?

PURDY. Yes, ma'am.

GRACE. To your *home*?

PURDY. I walked *here*.

GRACE. I – how silly this is becoming. You didn't go *home*?

PURDY. Have I upset you?

GRACE. No, it's – aren't you *expected*?

PURDY. Where?

GRACE. At your *home*?

PURDY. I don't know.

   Pause.

GRACE. Would you like to use the telephone?

PURDY. I've used it, thank you.

GRACE. You have.

PURDY. Yes, ma'am.

GRACE. So things are sorted out for you.

PURDY. I think they will be, yes.

   Pause.

GRACE. She is a good person, you know.

PURDY. Yes.

GRACE. A *kind* person. But certain situations, they lead to words which I cannot countenance. Things get said in the heat of a moment and then of course they can't be *unsaid*.

PURDY. No.

GRACE. Because of pain. Striking out with words to relieve one's pain. But of course the pain isn't *lessened* it is merely *redistributed*. And the people today who like to talk about how they *feel* and how important their *feelings* are, well, *pain* is a feeling, too. And the self-indulgence of these people and their *feelings*, their *whimsy* which they have the poor judgement to call *love* thereby casually *slandering* the word love itself, well, these people with their *feelings* need to remember that they are sharing their *feelings* in a way that causes *pain*. Pain is a feeling, too.

PURDY. Mm-hmm.

GRACE. We all have *feelings*. To suggest otherwise, even for a moment – well.

PURDY. To suggest – ?

GRACE. That one is *superior*.

PURDY. I see.

GRACE. In quality of *feeling*.

PURDY. I see.

GRACE. Superior *feelings*.

PURDY. Yes.

GRACE. We're not so different under the skin.

PURDY. That's been said.

GRACE. We know the difference between right and wrong.

PURDY. We do?

GRACE. As long as we listen to that still, small voice.

PURDY. Mm-hmm.

GRACE. As our Pastor says.

PURDY. Which voice?

GRACE. The one inside of us.

PURDY. The one that counsels some of us to love our enemies as we love ourselves?

GRACE. I believe so.

Pause.

PURDY. But isn't that the very same voice, which, with equal urgency, counsels *other* people that the proper thing to do is to *roast* their enemies' *bodies* and then say a prayer as they begin dining on their flesh?

Pause. GRACE is confused.

GRACE. I... think such people... are not really listening to the voice.

PURDY (*smiles*). Or perhaps they're hard of hearing.

GRACE. I don't know the word *de-veering*.

PURDY. *Hard of hearing*.

GRACE (*smiles*). I suppose so.

PURDY. And don't you feel superior to *them*?

GRACE. Superior… *to cannibals*?

PURDY. Yes.

Pause.

GRACE. I think I'll put my clothes on.

She doesn't move.

(*Kindly.*) Do you… need money?

PURDY. No, ma'am.

GRACE. Or food?

PURDY. I have the doughnuts.

GRACE. Money for a taxicab?

PURDY. I called for a taxicab.

GRACE (*relieved, realising*). Oh. *Ohhhhh*, I *see*. I see now. Good. Then you found our missing Yellow Pages?

PURDY. No, I have a card. From the train station.

GRACE. So that's clear now. So we're *waiting*, then. For the taxicab.

PURDY. Yes, ma'am.

GRACE. I see. That's all good, then.

PURDY. Yes.

GRACE. You see, I thought how could he not know Don and Marjorie Lively? How could he not know the Livelies? That struck me as unusual but of course the answer is that you're not from around here.

PURDY. No.

GRACE. You see, that explains a great deal.

PURDY. It must, yes.

GRACE. And that you would make a special trip. That you would go out of your way. Well. That speaks volumes.

PURDY. It seemed like a good idea.

GRACE. Lars was blessed with good friends.

PURDY. I hope so.

GRACE. So you'll be fine waiting here, then?

PURDY. Yes. Thank you.

GRACE *studies him for a moment, then exits.* PURDY *stares into space.*

(*Without difficulty.*) Sweater weather sweater weather sweater weather sweater weather.

He takes out a metal hip flask, opens it, and drinks.

THOR (*from the corner*). Thought you didn't drink.

PURDY. Forgot you were there.

THOR. But you do.

PURDY. Guess I wasn't a hundred per cent truthful about that.

THOR. I don't care.

Pause.

What does iconoclast mean?

PURDY. Do you know what it means?

THOR. Yes.

PURDY. Then why are you asking?

THOR. To see if you know.

PURDY. I know.

THOR. Why do you keep hanging around our house?

PURDY. I'm concerned.

THOR. What's your deal?

PURDY. I don't have a deal.

Pause.

THOR. You said a buried ordnance blew your hand off.

PURDY. Yes.

THOR. Isn't that the same as a landmine?

PURDY. Right.

THOR. Wouldn't a landmine blow off your *foot*?

PURDY. I was crawling.

THOR. Some people shoot their own hands off on purpose.

PURDY. Some do.

THOR. Why do they do that?

PURDY. I suppose they've lost faith in the objectives of the campaign.

THOR. Or because they're faggoty cowards.

Pause.

Are you a fag?

PURDY. No.

THOR. Are you a Communist?

PURDY. No.

THOR. I am.

PURDY. Okay.

THOR. What's so great about America?

PURDY. I didn't say it was.

THOR. You're the one fighting for it.

PURDY. Not any more.

Pause.

I suppose it's the best of several unappealing options.

THOR. I know how to make a flame-thrower.

PURDY. So you said.

CARLA appears from the hallway, wrapped in a blanket. She is extremely weak. She leans against a wall.

CARLA. I can help you shift.

PURDY stands. THOR exits to the bathroom.

If you can work the accelerator and the brake and the clutch then I can work the gear shift.

PURDY. I called a taxi.

CARLA. No no no. Wait. Where are you going?

PURDY. Wherever you want.

CARLA. Oh. Oh. Is it *here*?

PURDY. Not yet. Soon.

CARLA. Oh. Thank you. Thank you very much.

PURDY. Shh.

CARLA. Thank you.

Very carefully, CARLA makes her way to the sofa. PURDY tries to help.

PURDY. Can I get you something? Glass of water?

CARLA shakes her head.

Or a Coca-Cola? Some people, that settles their stomach. Or crackers. Some people put crackers in milk. Doesn't appeal to me.

THOR comes out of the bathroom with a hairspray can. He passes through to the kitchen without stopping.

Are you warm enough? Blanket's pretty thin. I could turn up the thermostat.

She does not respond.

Your son says he's a Communist.

CARLA *puts her hand to her head.*

Do you feel warm? You might be running a fever. Do you
mind if I – ?

He touches her forehead very gently.

Don't seem to be. But maybe a couple of aspirin. To be on
the safe side.

He looks at the clock.

Think your clock might be slow. (*Beat.*) Not that Marx
wasn't a great man. He was. In my opinion he just doesn't go
far enough. For example the classic analogy of private
property and theft. Not that is isn't *true*, but in his idealism
he misses the bigger picture, namely that all *happiness* is
theft. Because obviously there's a finite *amount* of
happiness. It doesn't keep *growing*, in fact it's *unhappiness*
that grows because the number of parties competing for the
limited supply of *happiness* keeps growing –

CARLA *covers her face.*

– exponentially. How's that pillow? Another? For back
support? Would that help? Or maybe if I just stopped *talking*.
That might be the thing.

CARLA. No.

PURDY. Oh. Uh –

CARLA. Keep talking.

PURDY. Okay.

CARLA. I like that you're talking.

PURDY. All right.

Pause.

CARLA. But now you *stopped*.

PURDY. Sorry.

CARLA. Anything.

PURDY. Uhhhh.

CARLA. A story.

PURDY. Self-conscious now.

CARLA. Or a joke.

PURDY. All right. Um. Let me see. I heard one. One was told to me. All right. A man – no, wait. A man? *Yes*, the man is a *butcher*, and he's working in his *butcher shop*. And he's working, I suppose is the idea. In the shop. And while working he accidentally backs into the… not the *slicer,* what's it called? The *meat grinder*. He's working and he backs into the meat grinder and the joke is that he gets a little *behind* in his work. More of a *pun*, really.

CARLA. Maybe a story.

PURDY. Let me think.

CARLA. Where did you grow up?

PURDY. A house like this.

CARLA. And what did you like to do?

PURDY. In the house?

CARLA. As a boy.

PURDY. Think about things.

CARLA. But what did you *do*?

PURDY. I spent a lot of time in my room. Reading.

CARLA. What books?

PURDY (*with a shrug*). Encyclopedia.

CARLA. What about your family?

PURDY. What about them?

CARLA. What were they like?

PURDY. Um. There was my mother. And my father.

CARLA. Did you have a brother?

PURDY. No.

CARLA. Maybe if you had.

PURDY. Maybe what?

CARLA. Wouldn't have spent so much time in your room.

PURDY. I liked being in my room.

CARLA. Still.

PURDY. What should I have done? Play *football*?

He takes out his flask and drinks. He offers it to CARLA.

CARLA. I don't drink any more.

PURDY. Neither do I.

She takes it from him and drinks. From outside, the sound of a car approaching. PURDY *exits quickly to the front door. The noise passes. He returns.*

(Re: the noise.) Garbage truck. *(A beat, then:)* I had a sister.

CARLA. Older?

PURDY. Younger.

CARLA. Did you like her?

PURDY. Everybody liked her. They still do.

CARLA. Where is she?

PURDY. Married. Participating in the marriage fantasy.

CARLA. Was she pretty?

PURDY. Very pretty.

CARLA. Beautiful?

PURDY. At the time. She was the first girl I ever kissed.

CARLA. For practice?

PURDY. Well, I was very quiet.

CARLA. You were *shy*.

PURDY. No. I could *move* quietly. I could walk into a room and leave it so that no one would know.

CARLA. Oh.

PURDY. Something I taught myself. I'd wait for my sister to go to sleep. I'd see her light go off. Then I'd wait thirty minutes and I'd walk down the hall very quietly. And I'd go into her room and kiss her. For practice, yes. For the future.

CARLA. She didn't wake up?

He sits again.

PURDY. Well, that's the funny thing. I wondered that myself. I mean, let's say you're asleep. You're fast asleep and someone comes into your room and kisses you. You'd wake up, wouldn't you? Of course you would. No matter how quiet they were. Of course you would. And in that case she was awake all along.

CARLA. Why don't you ask her?

PURDY. She'd never admit it.

CARLA. That she was awake?

PURDY. That she wanted to be kissed.

GRACE *enters. She is dressed.* CARLA *makes no attempt to hide the flask.*

GRACE. So this is where we are.

PURDY. Yes, ma'am.

GRACE. I put my clothes on because it seems that no one is going back to sleep.

PURDY. That seems reasonable.

She watches them.

GRACE. We're still waiting on that taxicab, then?

PURDY. Yes, ma'am.

GRACE. And I take it that's liquor that you're drinking.

PURDY. It is.

GRACE. I assume that belongs to you.

PURDY. Yes, ma'am.

GRACE. You see, I thought that we had decided that she was going back to bed.

PURDY. I don't know. I didn't take part in that decision.

GRACE. But it seems now she's changed her mind.

PURDY. Apparently she has.

GRACE. You offer a stronger incentive.

PURDY. I can't speak to that.

GRACE. You offer the incentive that she wants. That's fairly clear. I have to say I'm a bit surprised. I presumed better judgement on your part. But at least now she has what she wants.

PURDY. I can't speak for her, ma'am, only for myself.

GRACE. Well, let's ask her, then. Would you like to go back to bed, dear?

CARLA. No thanks.

GRACE. There we are. You're content to sit here, then. Your needs have been met.

CARLA. I'm not going to sit here.

GRACE. You're not.

CARLA. I already told you that.

GRACE. I see. (*To* PURDY.) So it wasn't necessarily for *yourself* that you called the taxicab, is that right?

PURDY. Not necessarily.

Pause.

GRACE. Well, I suppose that's another lesson for *me*, then. A lesson about my own irrelevance and obsolescence.

PURDY. Do you mean, because your beauty has faded?

GRACE. That's not what I mean. I didn't mean that at all. I mean because you seem to have everything she needs. You bring milk and you bring liquor and you bring the means to her freedom. So any further contribution from me seems irrelevant, doesn't it?

PURDY. I don't know.

GRACE. Why, *certainly* it does.

Pause.

And where will the two of go? In your *taxicab*?

PURDY. I believe that's up to her.

CARLA. Well, obviously somewhere where we can *fuck*, Grace, a warm place to *fuck*, because you know me I can't ever get *fucked* enough, so we'll just find a barn somewhere and he'll bend me over in the hay and *fuck* me like there's no tomorrow.

GRACE takes the keys from her pocket and places them on the table.

GRACE. All right then. Here are your car keys, dear. You do as you wish. I don't want it to be said that I interfered with your plans to hurt yourself once again.

CARLA (*to herself*). *Hurt* myself?

GRACE starts to go, stops.

GRACE (*to* PURDY). But I think if *that* is what you believe, Mr Purdy, if *that* is your notion of *beauty* then I must say I think that notion is very *immature*. Extremely so.

CARLA. I wasn't trying to *hurt* myself, Grace.

GRACE. And that's all I will say.

GRACE exits. CARLA calls after her.

CARLA. Why would I need to *hurt* myself? Huh? Hadn't that already been *accomplished*? (*To* PURDY.) I mean, if I want to spend my Fourth of July prancing around in a – Jesus, in a *bikini* and *high heels* trying to screw a couple of frat boys who only want to finish up the rest of the free beer and get the hell out of here, I mean – And then to wake up the next morning on the floor with a bottle because you needed to forget what an idiot you made of yourself, to wake up like that to the news that your *husband* – I mean, somewhere between the time that I'm standing next to my *dead husband* who is now on *exhibit*, between *that* and the point where I'm strapped down hands and feet in a *hospital* knocked out on *Thorazine* for nine, ten hours at a stretch just to be extra sure I don't *hurt myself*. *Somewhere* in there couldn't someone've, at *some point*, just walked over and said holy *shit*, lady. Wow, Carla, I gotta tell ya, all things considered you must feel really... *really*...

She can barely bring herself to say the word.

...*sad*.

Pause. PURDY *moves closer to her.*

PURDY. May I – I know this may not be the most – the optimal moment for such a – there's something I'd – I wonder if I could... speak to you... from my heart?

He sits. As he does so, we hear an audible fart. *Their eyes meet.* CARLA *laughs hard.*

CARLA. Did you *fart*?

PURDY (*grave*). It wasn't me.

She laughs harder.

It wasn't.

CARLA. You *farted*.

PURDY. I didn't.

CARLA. Must be the *doughnuts*.

PURDY. No, I – it wasn't –

CARLA. You need some Milk of Magnesia.

PURDY. Really.

She points to the sofa beneath PURDY.

CARLA. It's *Thor's*.

PURDY *pulls a whoopee cushion from under his seat*.

His father sends him things. Once a month. You're sitting in Grace's spot. Thor has her convinced that she has a little *problem*.

PURDY. I can see the humour in that.

CARLA. *Sent*, I should say. *Used to send*. From a novelty company. We still don't know what happened to the last package.

PURDY. So *Lars* used to send the jokes and novelties.

CARLA (*laughing*). Or did you actually *fart*?

PURDY. No. I was… attempting to say –

CARLA (*still laughing*). That you *farted*?

PURDY. No.

GRACE *enters. She carries another bottle of vodka, slightly smaller than the one previously seen. She places it on the table next to* CARLA's *keys*.

GRACE. This is from your car, dear. I return it to you.

CARLA *and* PURDY *start to smile*.

(*To* PURDY.) Your taxi service seems less than reliable. (*Beat, then, to* CARLA.) I hope you are *aware*, dear, that Mr Purdy, whose first name, I might add, we do not even know, that he is not a part of this community. He knows neither Don *nor* Marjorie Lively. He has never owned a *car*. These are the sort of things that I myself would want to know before I got into a taxicab with a person.

CARLA (*to* PURDY). What's your first name?

PURDY. It's *Nelson*.

CARLA. Could be worse.

PURDY. I could only have one hand.

CARLA *and* PURDY *try not to laugh.*

That's funny. I could never play the piano *before*.

They bust up laughing.

GRACE. I'll never understand why people of intelligence and originality need to drink. I'll never understand.

CARLA (*laughing, almost kindly*). Oh, *Grace*. That's easy. We drink because of people like *you*.

GRACE *exits to her room.* PURDY *and* CARLA *go on giggling for a long time. Then, silence.*

(*Finally.*) So what did he say about me?

PURDY. Who?

CARLA (*gives him a look*). Who do you *think*?

PURDY. He… didn't say anything.

CARLA. I want to know.

PURDY. Not to me.

CARLA (*laughs*). You didn't call him *Whitey* did you? Do they still call him that?

PURDY. Let's not talk about him.

CARLA. I want to know something he said.

PURDY. Uhhhh –

CARLA. Or a story. It's stupid of me. I know. Just a story. Not about me. I don't care about *me*. Just something stupid. A joke. (*Recalling* PURDY*'s attempt.*) Well, maybe not a joke – (*Continues.*)

PURDY (*as he rises, overlapping*). I need to see about that taxi.

CARLA. – something you did together. Oh oh oh. Did he tell you about *Mexico*? I know he told you about *Mexico*.

PURDY. I'm just going to call to check.

CARLA. I just want to know what *happ–*

She tries to stand but immediately doubles over. She grabs her stomach. Now the pain is much worse. She grips the arm of the sofa.

Owww. Owwwww. Shit. Owwwwww. Jesus. Owwwwwww. Why don't I know what happened? Owwwww why can't I *know what's happening?!! I don't know what's happening to me.*

PURDY (*attempting to touch her*). Shhh.

CARLA (*quietly, in tears, baffled*). I loved him so much.

PURDY. No.

CARLA. I miss him so much.

PURDY. Shhh.

GRACE comes out of her room and goes into THOR's room. PURDY hands CARLA some tissues. She blows her nose.

CARLA. Sorry.

GRACE passes through.

GRACE. Is Thor in here?

PURDY shakes his head.

He's not in his room.

She exits to the front door.

(*Calling, off.*) Thor?

PURDY (*looks at his watch*). Uhhh… I know… it would be premature of me, at this point, to introduce this topic, I mean, it's such an historically ill-defined and ambiguous notion, pathetic, really, the concept for which more lives have arguably been lost, next to the concept of *God*, this concept of *love* – a word best spoken through clenched teeth, however, given the urgent nature of your... predicament, I suppose one is forced to fall back on a word like *love* in order to explain their feelings and to – to – to...

CARLA stares at him blankly. PURDY sits by her side.

I'm not making much sense. I'm trying to say, in a roundabout way, and I do hope you won't *laugh* at me, it's rather important to me that you don't *laugh*, and I don't think you will because I'm fairly certain that the feeling is at least partially reciprocal, the feeling that I previously mentioned, but... Um. Do you have any idea what I am trying to say?

Pause. CARLA studies him.

CARLA. What predicament?

PURDY. What do you mean?

CARLA. You said given my predicament. What predicament?

PURDY. That wasn't really the point.

CARLA. No. What predicament are you talking about?

PURDY. Well. That you're going to have a child.

Pause.

CARLA. I didn't say that.

PURDY. No.

CARLA. Did Grace tell you that?

PURDY. No.

CARLA. Did *Thor*?

PURDY. No.

A longer pause.

CARLA. You didn't know my husband, did you?

PURDY. As I said, I was at the hospital *myself*.

CARLA. But you didn't.

PURDY. I had just lost my *hand*.

CARLA. But you didn't know him.

PURDY. It was late at night. Your door was open. I looked in. I
was very quiet. You spoke to me.

CARLA. About a jar full of snakes.

PURDY. You asked me to untie your hands. I said no one is
going to hurt you. And I didn't want you to hurt yourself.
You said to me go fuck yourself I'll hate you for as long as
you live.

CARLA. And you left the room. Then you left. Didn't you?

PURDY. You were so beautiful. You were the most beautiful
thing I'd ever seen.

A car horn sounds outside.

CARLA. So if Grace didn't tell you that. And if Thor didn't.
Then why would *you* think that?

PURDY. But it's true, isn't it? Isn't it true?

CARLA *understands. She begins laughing in disbelief.*

Please don't laugh at me. It's true, isn't it?

GRACE *enters. Her hearing aid is making its high-pitched
whining noise.*

GRACE. Your taxicab is here.

CARLA (*to* PURDY). No. *No*, as a matter of fact. It *isn't* true.

PURDY. Please don't laugh.

CARLA. I'm sorry. But *it isn't true*.

PURDY. Are you sure?

CARLA. *Oh* yes. I'm sure.

GRACE. I don't know how long the driver intends to wait.

CARLA. I'm *absolutely* sure.

PURDY (*turning to* GRACE). Ma'am?

GRACE. Yes?

CARLA. It's *definitely* not true.

PURDY. Your device.

> THOR *enters from the kitchen. He has the can of hairspray and a cigarette lighter.*

THOR. Watch this. Look.

PURDY. There's a noise.

GRACE. Is what?

THOR. Look over here.

PURDY. Your device is making a whistling noise.

GRACE. Divises *what*?

THOR. Look at this.

PURDY (*points to her head*). That.

GRACE (*thinking he is pointing behind her*). Where?

THOR. Hey.

PURDY. *It's making a noise.*

> *The horn honks again.*

THOR. *Hey!*

GRACE (*to* PURDY). Well, I don't know what you're *pointing* at.

THOR (*bellowing*). *WATCH THIS!! PAY ATTENTION!! I HAVE A FLAME-THROWER!!!!!*

> THOR *ignites the stream from the hairspray can. A burst of flame illuminates the room.*

GRACE. *THOR! NO FIRE IN THE HOUSE!! NEVER, EVER FIRE IN THE HOUSE!!!!*

PURDY *takes the can of hairspray from* THOR *and slaps him across the face.* THOR *stares back at him. Now* CARLA *stands. The blanket falls away. We can see clearly that the blanket and the back of her nightgown are wet with a generous amount of blood. The others see this.* CARLA *sees this too, and begins to laugh. The taxi horn sounds again.*

(*Quietly.*) That taxi is going to leave if no one stops it.

PURDY *approaches* GRACE. *He reaches to her and adjusts the hearing aid. The noise stops.* PURDY *exits.*

CARLA. I need my coat.

GRACE. I'll get it for you.

GRACE *goes to the closet.*

THOR (*quietly*). I've been waiting eight-and-a-half weeks for my package from the Johnson Smith Novelty Company and no one gives a shit if it comes or not.

GRACE (*to* CARLA). Here you are. Give me your arm.

CARLA (*almost giddy*). I'm *innocent*, Grace.

GRACE. There we go. Now the other.

THOR. No one pays the slightest attention.

GRACE (*to* CARLA). Let's get your slippers on.

THOR. No one cares. Money down the drain.

GRACE. Let me help you.

CARLA. I'm *innocent*.

GRACE. I do wish you had told me where you wanted to go.

THOR (*calm*). The package or the money. I don't care. I'd rather have the money.

GRACE (*also calm*). What package are you talking about?

THOR. From Johnson Smith Novelty Company.

GRACE. That came three weeks ago.

THOR. It did not.

GRACE. I put it in your closet.

THOR. Why didn't you tell me?

GRACE. I did tell you.

THOR. No you didn't.

GRACE. I thought I did.

THOR. Think harder next time.

GRACE. All right.

THOR. You're *senile*.

   THOR *exits to his room.*

GRACE. I'll get your scarf.

   She goes to the closet. PURDY *returns.*

PURDY. He's waiting.

GRACE. Thank you.

PURDY. Can I help?

GRACE. We're fine.

PURDY. I feel some... responsibility.

GRACE. We'll be fine.

CARLA (*to* GRACE). Will you come with me?

GRACE. Well. Mr Purdy called the taxi.

CARLA. I'd prefer it.

PURDY. Either way.

GRACE. All right. I'd be happy to.

   GRACE *goes to the closet for her coat.* CARLA *takes
   another look at* PURDY. *Now she laughs hard.* GRACE
   returns.*

Let's tuck your scarf in.

CARLA. What about the Pastor?

GRACE. We'll call and reschedule.

CARLA grabs her stomach again. GRACE helps her toward the door.

CARLA. I'm innocent, Grace.

GRACE. I know, dear.

CARLA. I wasn't sure.

GRACE. Of course you are.

CARLA. I didn't know.

GRACE. I never said otherwise.

They are gone. The sun has risen. Sunlight slants across the room. PURDY stands in the middle of the room, unsure of his next move. We hear the taxi drive away. Then THOR re-enters with his package. He and PURDY stare at each other for a moment. PURDY moves first, and sits in the centre of the sofa.

So THOR goes to the stereo and drops the needle on the record. He, too, sits on the sofa. He stares at PURDY as the music returns, as loud as before.

PURDY stands and turns the music off, then returns to his position on the sofa. THOR watches him. A pause, then.

THOR. You saw a dog eat a person?

PURDY (*eyes closed*). Mm-hm.

THOR. Where?

PURDY. There was a village. It had been burned the week before. We were on patrol. Came to this village. Behind this hut there was a woman on the ground. A dog had its head up inside her ribcage. Hungry I guess. Heard us coming. Looked up. Scared. Took a shot at it. Missed. It ran away with something in its mouth. Something purple. Looked like a heart. But of course a heart doesn't often conform to the traditionally accepted shape. Actually looked more like a football. But I think it was a heart. Could have been a kidney.

THOR *reaches over and takes the watch off of* PURDY*'s wrist, begins changing the time.*

THOR (*as he resets the time*). There's this girl in my class this girl Tammy McFadden. She's a whore. She has big tits and acne. My friend Ricky Purzer says she lets guys finger her in the utility room for five dollars. She goes around telling everyone that she loves me so I'm gonna take her to the woods by the creek behind the Methodist church and I'm gonna dig a punji trap. And when she follows me into the woods she won't be looking where she's going and she'll fall in the trap and then she'll die.

He replaces PURDY*'s watch.*

PURDY. Your mother looked so beautiful lying there. She was the most beautiful thing I'd ever seen.

THOR *opens the box and places it between them. They both reach in. They pull out various novelty items and place them on the coffee table. Finally,* PURDY *pulls out a rubber severed hand as* THOR *extracts a can with the words 'Peanut Brittle' on it.*

THOR. Look. Have some candy. Peanut Brittle.

PURDY. You first.

THOR. I'm gonna have some.

PURDY. Go ahead.

THOR. Don't mind if I do.

PURDY. All right.

THOR. I'm gonna do it.

PURDY. Okay.

THOR. Watch. Here it goes.

THOR *unscrews the top of the can. Three 'snakes' jump out.*

That was stupid.

The two of them look at the snakes littering the floor.

Once the snakes are out of the can, how do you get them back in again?

PURDY *stares at* THOR *as the lights fade to black. No music.*

End of play.

A Nick Hern Book

Purple Heart first published in Great Britain as a paperback original in 2013 by Nick Hern Books Limited, The Glasshouse, 49a Goldhawk Road, London W12 8QP, in association with the Gate Theatre, London

Purple Heart copyright © Bruce Norris 2005, revised 2013

Bruce Norris has asserted his right to be identified as the author of this work

Cover image: © Bill Owens (www.billowens.com)
Cover design: Ned Hoste, 2H

Typeset by Nick Hern Books, London
Printed in Great Britain by Mimeo Ltd, St Ives, Cambs, PE27 3LE

A CIP catalogue record for this book is available from the British Library

ISBN 978 1 84842 308 4